Michael Jackson's
COMPLETE GUIDE TO
SINGLE MALT
SCOTCH

Michael Jackson's
COMPLETE GUIDE TO
SINGLE MALT SCOTCH

A CONNOISSEUR'S GUIDE TO THE SINGLE MALT WHISKIES OF SCOTLAND

SECOND EDITION

RUNNING PRESS
PHILADELPHIA, PENNSYLVANIA

Library of Congress Cataloging-in-Publication Number
91-53205

ISBN 1-56138-081-4

Published in the U.S. in 1990, 1991 by Running Press Book Publishers

First published in Great Britain as
Michael Jackson's Malt Whisky Companion,
Copyright © 1989 Dorling Kindersley Limited
Text copyright © 1989, 1990, 1991 Michael Jackson

Designed and edited by Melissa Denny of Diptych

Managing editor Jemima Dunne

Managing art editor Derek Coombes

Cover design by Toby Schmidt

Cover illustration by Liz Vogdes

This book may be ordered by mail from the publisher.
Please add $2.50 for postage and handling.
But try your bookstore first!

Running Press Book Publishers
125 South Twenty-second Street
Philadelphia, Pennsylvannia 19103

Printed and bound by Wing King Tong, Hong Kong

CONTENTS

INTRODUCTION

T O HAVE CREATED the pleasure of the single-malt Scotch is a magnificent achievement. How odd, then, to keep it almost a secret, which the Scots have done for decades. There is a charm to the reserve of the Highlander and Islander, but thank heavens they let slip the gift of single malts.

I stumbled upon my first malt as an 18-year-old, and have in the three decades since regarded Scotland as an Aladdin's cave of alcohols. Some would still keep this secret, but that would cause the source to dry up through neglect. Others have drawn attention to the history and romance of the malts, and even – too briefly – given attention to their character. That, to me, is what matters.

The single malts are the most natural of spirits, formed more than any other by their environment. For the same reason, they are the most individualistic. One arouses the appetite before dinner, another soothes the digestion; one likes to follow a round of golf, another prefers a book at bedtime. No other spirit offers such diversity of character. Among the others, Armagnac has perhaps the greatest diversity, but is still primarily an after-dinner drink.

Even the same single malt may evolve in character with age and strength, and according to the type of wood in which it has come to maturity. The products of more than a hundred malt distilleries have at one time or another in recent years been made available as single malts. Some are available at only one standard age, others are "vintage" dated, with the year of distillation and sometimes of bottling. Some are available in a wide variety of ages, and others at more than one strength. Some single malts can currently be found in half a dozen or more bottlings.

Which is best? Some are clearly more characterful than others, but they also vary in dryness and sweetness, fullness and lightness, crispness and roundness, assertiveness and elegance; in nose, body, palate and finish. A light, dry aromatic malt may be better before dinner; a fuller, sweeter, rounder one afterwards. A soft malt may be a restorative after a walk; a heavier, smokier one might be better at bedtime.

What follows is the most extensive review ever undertaken of the character of single malts. I make no apology for having become so excited about some of them. They have that effect. Some that I have loved for decades still surprise and enchant me in the cocktail bar, at the dinner table or even at bedtime, and I shall continue to explore their charms.

The origin of the spirit

It is commonly understood that warm countries grow fruits, especially the grape, from which to ferment wines and distil brandies. It is less well appreciated that some of the cooler nations cultivate grain, especially barley, which they ferment to make beer and distil to create whisky.

What all whiskies have in common is that they retain the character of the original grain., They are not distilled to faint-hearted tastelessness, like the Western style of vodka. Nor are they flavoured with herbs, spices or berries, like aquavit, gin or many of the original Slavic vodkas.

The art of distillation is believed to have been discovered in the Orient, perhaps in China, to have been brought West by the Arabs, and to have been introduced by the Moors into Spain where it was used in the production of perfumes and medicines. The first distilling of alcohol in Europe was in grape-growing countries.

Distilling seems to have been established in Scotland in the 1400s, though it may have been practised in Ireland earlier. By the mid 1700s, a distinction was made in Scotland between spirits flavoured with herbs and spices, and "plain malt".

Spirits in general have been known in several parts of Europe as "the water of life": in Latin, "aqua vitae"; in French, "eau-de-vie"; in Scottish and Irish Gaelic, "uisge beatha" or "usquebaugh", among other spellings. These Gaelic names, sounding to the English-speaker like "uishgi", were corrupted to "whisky".

Landseer's The Highland Whisky Still, *painted in the 1820s, captures clearly the atmosphere of an early illegal still or bothy.*

SINGLE MALT:
THE APPELLATION

The term SINGLE has a very clear and precise meaning. It indicates that the whisky was made in only one distillery, and has not been blended with any from elsewhere.

The term MALT indicates the raw material: barley malt, and no other grain or fermentable material; infused with water, fermented with yeast and distilled in a pot.

The term SCOTCH means that the whisky was distilled and matured in the country whose name it bears. Outside Britain, there is one single malt (but not Scotch) made in Ireland. There are also three or four single malts (but not Scotch) made in Japan.

A SINGLE MALT SCOTCH must fulfill all three requirements. It must be the product of only one distillery; it must be made exclusively from barley malt; and it must be made in Scotland.

There has been the odd occasion when the product of one run of the still has been aged in identical casks, then bottled. This has been described as a "Single/Single". That is not the normal procedure. Although a single malt always comes from one distillery, whisky from half-a-dozen production batches over a two-year period, aged in different casks, might be married in wood for several weeks and then fed into one bottling run. The age on the bottle will represent the youngest whisky inside.

Some single malts are labelled as "Pure Malt". However, this term is also often used to indicate a vatting together of malt whiskies made in several distilleries. This type of whisky is technically known as vatted malt. It may also be labelled simply as a "Malt Whisky", or if it comes from the right country as a "Malt Scotch Whisky" or "Scotch Malt Whisky". Although such bottlings are perfectly legitimate, and often excellent products, their labels usually identify only the brand-owner or blender, and not the distilleries.

A blended Scotch commonly contains about 40 percent malt; the odd one contains more than 60 percent. The cheaper blends contain much less. The deluxe blends are likely to contain a good proportion of well-matured malt, which is why some carry an age statement. Once again the age statement reflects the age of the youngest whisky.

Only single malts that bear the distillery names or are distillery brands are reviewed here. Among the 100-odd distilleries discussed in the book, a number are temporarily or permanently closed, but their single malts are still available.

WHY SINGLE MALTS DIFFER

All single malts are individuals, in some cases as distinct from each other as they are from the blends they inhabit. But before looking at the variables that conspire to produce such a diverse family, a brief reminder of the processes used in the creation of *all* malts might be helpful.

MALTING: Barley has to be partially germinated before it can release its fermentable sugars. It is soaked in water until it begins to sprout, then this is arrested by drying the grains over heat. This steeping and drying process is called *malting*. Traditionally, the Scots dried their malt over a peat fire, which gives Scotch its characteristic smokiness. A proportion of peat is still burned during malting.

MASHING: To complete the conversion of starch into fermentable sugars, the malt (which has been milled after malting) is mixed with warm water in a vessel called a mash-tun. The liquid drained off is known as *wort*.

FERMENTATION: The sugars in the wort are now turned into alcohol during fermentation, which takes place with the addition of yeast, in a fermentation vessel.

DISTILLATION: This is the boiling of the fermented wort, in a pot-still. Because alcohol boils more rapidly than water, the spirit is separated as a vapour and collected as it condenses back to alcohol.

MATURATION: All malts are matured in oak barrels, for a legal minimum of three years, though usually much longer.

Germinating malt must be turned, left, *to aerate the grains. In the mash tun,* above, *rotating "blades" churn the malt.*

THE POT-STILL

A single malt is distilled in traditional vessels that resemble a copper kettle or pot. These are known as pot-stills. Most other types of whisky are made predominantly from other grains, in a more modern system: a continuous still, shaped like a column.

Much of the flavour of the malt is retained in pot distillation because this old fashioned system is inherently inefficient. A column system can distil more thoroughly, but makes for a less flavourful spirit. Blended Scotch whiskies contain a proportion of pot-still malt, leavened with continuous-still whisky made from cheaper, unmalted grains.

The shape of the still

The pot-still is a vessel shaped by a coppersmith, and in no two distilleries is it identical. Some Scottish malt distilleries trace their history from the late 1700s, and many from the early and mid 1800s. Over the years, each distillery has been reluctant to change the shape of its stills. As they wear out, they are replaced by new ones of the same design. If the last still was dented, the distillery may get the same depression hammered into the new still.

The reason for this is that every variation in the shape of the still affects the character of the product. A small, squat still produces a heavy, oily, creamy spirit. In a large still, some of the vapours condense before they have left the vessel, fall back and are redistilled. This means that tall stills produce lighter, cleaner, spirits.

Most malts are run through two linked pot-stills: the wash-still and the spirit-still. In some Lowland distilleries, and in Ireland, a system of three pot-stills is used.

Glenmorangie's pot stills, left, *are the tallest in Scotland. The Macallan's stills,* above, *are the smallest on Speyside.*

THE INFLUENCES OF LOCATION

The two spirits most often compared for their regionality are Cognac and single-malt Scotch. In Cognac, the regions of production are contiguous, and stretch about 150 km (90 miles) from end to end. The single malts spread over an area about 450 km (300 miles) from one end to the other, including most of Scotland. Cognacs are usually blends; a single malt bears the regional character of just one distillery.

Water
Producers of several types of drink talk in hushed tones of the importance of their water. Nowhere is it more genuinely significant than in single-malt Scotches. The water used in the single malts is usually not treated, and each distillery's supply has its own personality.

Water that rises from granite has its own clean softness. If it rises from – or flows over – peat it will pick up that character. In the Highlands, much water used in distilling rises from granite and flows over peat.

The water may make its presence felt twice. It is used to steep the grains in the handful of distilleries that have their own maltings, and then again in the infusion that precedes fermentation and distillation. Peaty water can impart a smoky character to a single-malt Scotch. So, of course, does the extent to which peat is used in the kilning of the malt. These two elements of peatiness each have their own character, and the interplay between them is a part of the complexity of many single malts. In some instances, the water may impart a smokiness even where only a medium-peated malt has been used.

Soil
The soil will affect not only the water, but also the character of the local peat. If malting is done at the distillery, local peat will be used in the kilning. The age of peat deposits, and their degree of grass-root or heather character, will have its own influence on the malt.

Micro-climate
Although similar yeasts (of broadly the ale type) are used throughout the malt distilling industry, each tun room (fermentation hall) produces its own characteristics. This may vary according to the material from which the fermenting vessels are made, with wood perhaps harbouring its own resident microflora, but it is also influenced by the micro-climate in and around the distillery.

Temperature

A cold location makes for low temperature spring waters.
When very cold water is available for use in the coils that
condense the spirit, and the ambient temperature is low, that
seems to produce an especially rich, clean, whisky. Distilleries
in shaded, mountain, locations are noted for this characteristic.
The oak casks used during the maturation of the whisky
expand and contract according to the temperature. The wider
the local extremes of temperature, the more this happens.

Air

This is a very significant factor. As the casks "breathe", they
inhale the local atmosphere. The more traditional type of
maturation warehouse has an earth floor, and often a damp
atmosphere. The influence of this is especially noticeable in
distilleries that are close to the sea. Often, their maturation
warehouses are at the water's edge, washed by high seas. Some
single malts, especially those from rocky coasts, have a
distinctly briny or seaweedy character.

THE CLASSIC REGIONS

Like wines – and many other drinks – the single malts of
Scotland are grouped by region. As with wines, these regions
offer a guideline rather than a rule. Within Bordeaux, a
particular Pomerol, for example, might have a richness more
reminiscent of Burgundy; similar comparisons can be made
in Scotland. The regions in Scotland have their origins in the
regulation of licences and duties, but they do also embrace
certain characteristics.

The Lowlands

The Lowlands tend to produce whiskies in which the softness
of the malt itself is more evident, untempered by Highland
peatiness or coastal brine and seaweed. The Lowlands is
defined by a line following old county boundaries and running
from the Clyde estuary to the river Tay. The line swings north
of Glasgow and Dumbarton and runs to Dundee and Perth.

The Highlands

The Highlands is by far the bigger region, and inevitably
embraces wide variations. The western part of the Highlands, at
least on the mainland, has only a few, scattered, distilleries, and
it is difficult to generalise about their character. If they have
anything in common, it is a rounded, firm, dry character, with
some peatiness. The far north of the Highlands has several
whiskies with a notably heathery, spicy, character, probably

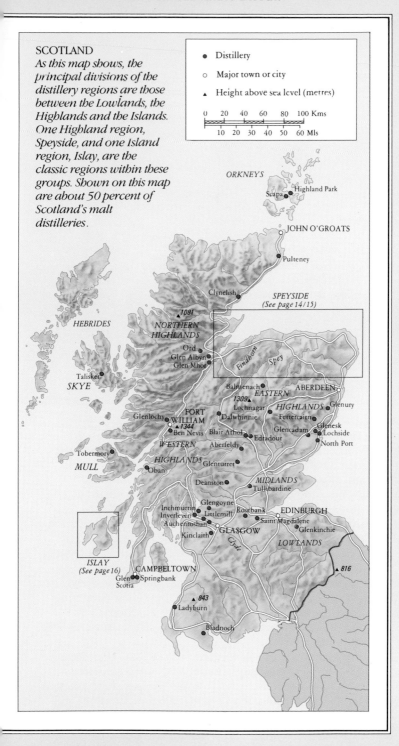

SCOTLAND
As this map shows, the principal divisions of the distillery regions are those between the Lowlands, the Highlands and the Islands. One Highland region, Speyside, and one Island region, Islay, are the classic regions within these groups. Shown on this map are about 50 percent of Scotland's malt distilleries.

● Distillery

○ Major town or city

▲ Height above sea level (metres)

0 20 40 60 80 100 Kms

10 20 30 40 50 60 Mls

ORKNEYS

Scapa   Highland Park

JOHN O'GROATS

Pulteney

Clynelish

SPEYSIDE
(See page 14/15)

HEBRIDES

▲ *1081*

NORTHERN
HIGHLANDS

Ord
Glen Albyn
Glen Mhor

Findhorn   *Spey*

Talisker

SKYE

Balmenach

ABERDEEN

EASTERN

▲ *1309*

HIGHLANDS   Glenury

Lochnagar
Fettercairn

Glenlochy   FORT
WILLIAM   Dalwhinnie
Glencadam   Glenesk
▲ *1344*   Lochside
Ben Nevis   Blair Athol   North Port

WESTERN   Edradour

HIGHLANDS   Aberfeldy

Tobermory

MULL   Glenturret

Oban

Deanston   MIDLANDS

Tullibardine

Glengoyne

Inchmurrin   Littlemill   Rosebank   EDINBURGH
Inverleven
Auchentoshan   Saint Magdalene

Kinclaith   GLASGOW   Glenkinchie

Clyde   LOWLANDS

ISLAY
(See page 16)   CAMPBELTOWN

Glen   Springbank
Scotia

▲ *816*

▲ *843*

Ladyburn

Bladnoch

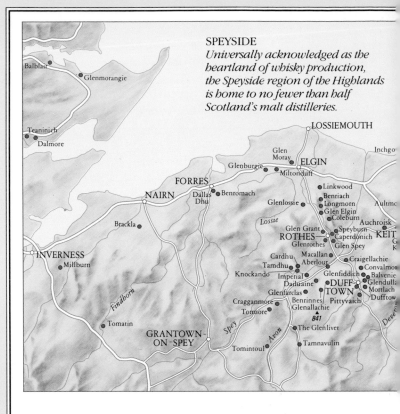

SPEYSIDE
Universally acknowledged as the heartland of whisky production, the Speyside region of the Highlands is home to no fewer than half Scotland's malt distilleries.

deriving both from the local soil and the coastal location of all distilleries. The more sheltered East Highlands and the Midlands of Scotland (sometimes described as the South Highlands) have a number of notably fruity whiskies.

None of these Highland areas are officially regarded as regions, but the area between them, known as Speyside, is universally acknowledged as a heartland of malt distillation. This area, between the cities of Inverness and Aberdeen, sweeps from granite mountains down to fertile countryside, where barley is among the crops. It is the watershed of a system of rivers, the principal among which is the Spey. Although it is not precisely defined, Speyside is commonly agreed to extend at least from the river Findhorn to the Deveron. Within this region are several other rivers, notably including the Livet.

The *Speyside* single malts are noted in general for their elegance and complexity, and often a refined smokiness. Beyond that, they have two extremes: the big, sherryish type, as typified by The Macallan, Glenfarclas and Aberlour; and the lighter, more subtle, style.

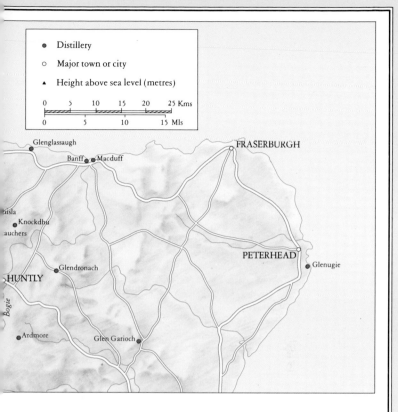

Within Speyside, the river *Livet* is so famous that its name is borrowed by some whiskies from far beyond its glen. Only one may call itself The Glenlivet; only two more are produced in the valley, and a further one in the parish. These are all delicate malts, and it could be more tentatively argued that other valleys have malts that share certain characteristics.

The Highland region includes a good few coastal and island malts, but one peninsula and just one island have been of such historical importance in the industry that they are each regarded as being regions in their own right.

Campbeltown

On the peninsula called the Mull of Kintyre, Campbeltown once had about 30 distilleries. Today, it has only two. One of these, Springbank, produces two different single malts. This apparent contradiction is achieved by the use of a lightly peated malt in one and a smokier kilning in the other.

The Campbeltown single malts are very distinctive, with a briny character. Although there are only three of them, they are still considered to represent a region in their own right.

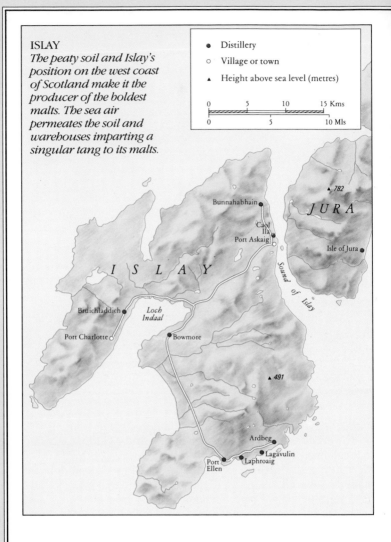

ISLAY
The peaty soil and Islay's position on the west coast of Scotland make it the producer of the boldest malts. The sea air permeates the soil and warehouses imparting a singular tang to its malts.

- ● Distillery
- ○ Village or town
- ▲ Height above sea level (metres)

0   5   10   15 Kms

0   5   10 Mls

▲ 782

JURA

Bunnahabhain

Caol Ila
Port Askaig

Isle of Jura ●

I S L A Y

Sound of Islay

Bruichladdich ●   Loch Indaal

Port Charlotte ○   ● Bowmore

▲ 491

Ardbeg ●
● Lagavulin
Port Ellen ●   ● Laphroaig

Islay

Pronounced "eye-luh", this is the greatest of whisky islands: much of it deep with peat, lashed by the wind, rain and sea in the inner Hebrides. It is only 25 miles long, but has no fewer than eight distilleries, although not all are working. Its single malts are noted for their seaweedy, iodine-like, phenolic character. A dash of Islay malt gives the unmistakable tang of Scotland to many blended whiskies.

MATURATION

Wooden casks were originally used simply as containers, and the ability of spirits to develop with age and according to the type of wood they matured in was discovered only by accident. Although the benefits of maturation are said to have been known to wealthy cellar-owners since the early days of distilled spirits in Britain, whisky was not systematically aged until the late 1800s.

Age

As laws were shaped to define whisky, in the early 1900s, a minimum maturation period of three years was laid down, and this measure still applies. A bottled single malt is unlikely to be marketed at this age. In Italy, where single malts are in great demand at competitive prices, five-year-olds sell well, but these are still on the young side. A young malt still tastes spirity, and may have an excessive "pear-drop" character. With maturity, it will gain roundness, depth and length of finish.

From five years onward, most malts begin to achieve maturity, though some progress faster than others. In general, the lighter malts mature fastest. A malt may also develop quickly at some stages, level off for a time, then sometimes start to develop again. Each has its own, different, life-cycle. Some are in good shape at eight or 10 years, others at 12, which is a popular standard. Fifteen years seems a particularly fine age for many single malts. Some continue to mature at 25, or even 50, though often with some woodiness.

Once bottled, a whisky will no longer improve. In theory, it will not deteriorate, either, but there is no sense in keeping bottled malts for long periods. Despite its great strength, whisky can gradually "collapse" if a small amount is left for a long time in an opened bottle.

Choice of wood

In the days when Spain shipped large quantities of sherry in the cask to England, the importers found a ready market for the empty barrels by selling them to the Scots as maturation vessels for whisky. At that time, a wide variety of casks were in circulation: some had been used for the primary fermentation of sherry, others in the solera system of maturation; some for fino, others for oloroso or amontillado; some merely for transport or storage. Today, because wood is used less, some distilleries actually commission their own barrels from cooperages in Spain and then lend them to bodegas in Spain, before shipping them to Scotland. The bodega gets use of the barrels free and the distillery has them "wined".

The influence of sherry casks provides a richness, roundness and depth in single-malt Scotch. This was discovered by chance, in what one producer calls a "sublime accident" Some purists feel that sherry ageing is essential in the production of a true, traditional single malt. Macallan is the only distillery to use exclusively sherry wood. It fills its casks twice, then disposes of them. Some distilleries go on to a third and fourth fill.

Another approach is to use casks that have previously been used to mature Bourbon. The rules concerning Bourbon say that it must be matured for not less than four years in "new" oak. This means that the casks can be used only once for Bourbon. As several Bourbon producers are under the same ownership as Scottish malt distilleries, there was a tidy logic to this arrangement.

New oak imparts the vanilla-like character that is a defining element in Bourbon but which would overwhelm a Scottish malt. Once most of this character has been given up to the Bourbon, it will have only a slight influence on a subsequent fill of Scottish malt.

Both Spain and Kentucky use only oak for their casks. Spain uses both its own oak, from Galicia, and some from the United States. Spanish oak has a more resiny character, especially if it grew in the mountains. American oak is finer grained, harder and slower to mature the whisky.

Many distilleries have an assortment of different generations of sherry and Bourbon casks, and orchestrate these in the final vatting of their single malt. There may well be malts in a single bottle aged in four or five "woods".

Oak staves are steamed and shaped into Bourbon casks, above left. *These are briefly charred,* above right, *before being hand-finished.*

Alcohol content/proof

All spirits are distilled at a higher alcohol content than makes for a pleasant drink. In order that the character of the original material be retained, the law insists that Scotch whisky be distilled at a percentage of alcohol by volume that is clearly under 95 (to ensure this, 94.8 is specified). In practice, malts come off the still in the range of 75-60. At the higher end, malts may be very slightly reduced with water before being put into the cask. Typically, a malt goes into the cask in the mid 60s. Further changes of alcohol content occur naturally inside the cask during maturation. In a dry atmosphere, evaporation will affect the bulk of the content of the cask; in damp surroundings, alcohol will be lost.

Single malts sold at "cask strength" range in alcohol content from just under 60 to just over 50. Even with a dash of water, a malt in this range will retain more power and texture than one at a standard strength. Most single malts, in common with other spirits, are further reduced with water before being bottled, and marketed at 43 in some international markets and 40 as a standard.

Alcohol by volume is the easiest measure to understand, and the system that is now standard throughout Europe. Forty percent alcohol by volume is the equivalent of 70 proof in the complicated system previously used in Britain, or 80 proof in the American system.

The Macallan's production director samples sherry in a bodega; the casks labelled "MG" will be used to mature the Macallan malt.

A-Z
OF SINGLE MALTS

Over the next 200 pages is the most comprehensive survey yet produced of the characteristics of different single malt Scotches. I have discussed in alphabetical order every distillery whose malts can be found in the bottle: more than a hundred in all. Where a distillery's malts can be sampled in two or three (or even eight or nine) different ages or strengths, I have made notes across the range. I have also given each example a score (see p. 23 for scoring system).

New ages and "vintages"

Since the first edition of this book was produced, many distilleries have added to, or changed, the range of ages they make available. Some did not previously make available their malts as bottled singles at all, and now do. The tasting notes in this edition attempt to cover earlier versions that might still be found on the shelf, together with all of the additions. Independent bottlers sometimes release malts from only one or two casks at a time, so their selections change even faster. The tasting notes here offer a representative review of recent independent bottlings.

More than a third of the tasting notes in the book are new. The malts described were all tasted specifically for this book, though my notes also take into account my previous samplings in other situations, including various panel judgings.

New malts

In 1990, the first new distillery in a decade and a half was opened by the owners of Glenfiddich and Balvenie. The new distillery, Kininvie, is next door to its older brothers in Dufftown. Kininvie's whisky, fresh from the still, seems to have an earthy-fruity character of its own, and some of the sweetness of Balvenie. In something between five and ten years, perhaps there will be a mature version to taste from the bottle.

The opening of Kininvie was the most dramatic evidence of the renaissance in malt distilling at the beginning of the 1990s. The reopening of more than a dozen "silent" distilleries around that time told the same story. There are currently more than a hundred malt distilleries in working order in Scotland, of which all but half a dozen are in operation. The others are held in reserve.

Among working distilleries are a handful whose malt whisky seems not yet to have found its way into the bottle as a single: Alt-a-Bhaine, Braes of Glenlivet, Mannochmore and Strathmill. Several distilleries that closed some years ago bequeathed stocks of maturing whisky that are occasionally bottled, and they are among those reviewed in the pages that follow.

"Official" and "unofficial" bottlings

Since the days when they were a farmhouse industry, some distilleries have never offered their whiskies in the bottle as singles, but have preferred to sell them in the cask, often by way of whisky brokers, to merchants and blenders. This was traditionally the way industry operated, and is how a malt from a distillery identified by name may find its way into bottlings with a variety of merchants' labels.

Some distilleries are happy for this to continue: to sanction merchants to do their own bottling. Others feel that, with so much maturing whisky already in the hands of middlemen, there is nothing they can do to stop perfectly legitimate but "unofficial", bottlings. Others have in recent years bought back supplies of their whisky from brokers in order to control their own bottlings.

In choosing casks for bottling, a distillery will try to ensure a consistency in its product. Independent bottlings are more variable, according to the character of the casks available. This can confuse the consumer, but that is a small price to pay for the service given to malt-lovers by the independent bottlers: over the years, the independents have been the sole source of many malts.

Similar labels

Many of the labels in this book are similar. One reason for this is that each independent bottler has its own label design which it uses for the different malts it offers. Gordon and MacPhail bottles its rarer malts under the rubric Connoisseurs Choice, with a buff label, trimmed in orange, and featuring a detail of a map of Scotland. This label will be used for various malts, from Aberfeldy and Balmenach to Teaninich and Tomatin. Most Cadenhead labels look similar, whatever the distillery named, and the same is true of wine merchants like Avery's, Reid's and Berry Brothers.

The other reason for similar labels is that in 1990/91 United Distillers began a series of bottlings of their previously unreleased single malts. These malts all have labels depicting local flora and fauna, and are intended primarily for sale in the area of each distillery – though some have already been marketed nationally in Britain.

A GUIDE TO THE TASTING NOTES

A tasting note cannot be definitive, but it can be a useful guide: if you are looking for a light dry malt, do not choose this one, pick the next. If you wanted something rich and sherryish, here is the one. This is the spirit, so to speak, in which I have over the years attempted to describe the character of beer, and in this work, single malts. To give you as full a picture as possible, the tasting notes give details of COLOUR, NOSE, BODY, PALATE and FINISH for every malt in the A-Z.

Colour
The natural colour of a malt matured in plain wood is a very pale yellow. Darker shades, ranging from amber to ruby to deep brown, can be imparted by sherry wood. Some distilleries use casks treated with concentrated sherry, and this can cause a caramel-like appearance and palate. I do not suggest that one colour is in itself better than another, though a particular subtle, or profound, hue can heighten the pleasure of a fine malt. It is, after all, a drink to contemplate.

Nose
Some lovers of wines and spirits feel that single malts are unusual among drinks in the honesty of their aroma. This school says that, in malts, the nose gives an accurate indication of the palate. I do not agree. In my perception, characteristics in the nose can move into the background of the palate, then re-emerge in the finish.

Body
Lightness or fullness might be required on different occasions, but body and texture (sometimes known as "mouth feel") are distinct features in the overall character of each malt.

Palate
In the enjoyment of any complex drink, each sip will offer new aspects of the taste. Even one sip will gradually unfold a number of taste characteristics in different parts of the mouth over a period of, say, a minute. This is notably true of single malts. Some present a very extensive development of palate. A taster working with an unfamiliar malt may go back to it several times over a period of days, in search of its full character. I have adopted this technique in my tastings for this book.

Finish

In all types of alcoholic drink, the "finish" is a part of the experience. In some drinks, including most single malts, it is more than a simple aftertaste, however important that may be. It is a crescendo, followed by a series of echoes. When I leave the bottle, I like to be whistling the tune.

THE SCORING SYSTEM

Whatever the arguments about their relative prices, no-one denies that a Château Latour is more complex than a mass-market table wine. Even within the range of fine wine, such judgements can be made clearly enough. The fine wines of the whisky world are the single malts. Some malts are made to higher standards than others, and some are more distinctive than their neighbours. This cannot honestly be obscured by the producers' blustery arguments about "personal taste". Neither, though, can the excellence of such complex products be measured very satisfactorily. The scoring system I have developed and used in the A-Z section is therefore intended as nothing more than a guide to the status of the malts reviewed.

The distillery rating ☆☆☆☆☆

The distilleries are each given a star rating of between one and five stars. These ratings represent my judgement of the "ambitions" of a particular distillery. One star indicates that a malt is not usually intended to be available as a single; two stars represent distilleries that have not seriously entered the market for singles. Three stars suggest a producer of well-made malts, while four stars suggest something out of the ordinary. Five means that the distillery produces a malt that is a classic example of the regional style.

The individual score SCORE 100

Each individual tasting note is given a numerical score out of 100. Of these scores, one in the 50s indicates, in my view, a malt lacking in balance or character and which – in fairness – was probably never meant to be bottled as a single. The 60s suggests an enjoyable but unexceptional malt. Anything in the 70s, especially beyond 75, is well worth tasting. The 80s are distinctive and exceptional. The 90s are the greats.

ABERFELDY

Distillery rating ☆☆ **Producer** United Distillers
Region Highland **District** Midlands

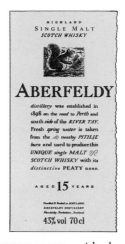

HIGHLAND
SINGLE MALT
SCOTCH WHISKY

ABERFELDY

distillery was established in
1898 *on* the *road* to *Perth* and
south *side* of the *RIVER TAY*.
Fresh *spring water* is taken
from the nearby *PITILIE
burn* and used to produce this
*UNIQUE single MALT
SCOTCH WHISKY* with its
distinctive PEATY nose.

A G E D **15** Y E A R S

Distilled & Bottled in SCOTLAND
ABERFELDY DISTILLERY
Aberfeldy, Perthshire, Scotland
43% vol 70cl

AN AFTER-DINNER MALT, with the sweetish, perfumed, character that often seems to occur in whiskies from this part of Scotland. The oldest buildings at Aberfeldy date from 1896, though there was much reconstruction and expansion in the 1960s and 1970s. The distillery is in the Grampian mountain resort and market town of Aberfeldy, high on the river Tay. The malt whisky is a component of Dewar's. Aberfeldy was first officially bottled as a single in 1991.

ABERFELDY 15-year-old, 43 vol (cask sample)
Colour Amber.
Nose Barley-grain. Heathery. Incense-like. Very faint smoky peatiness.
Body Soft, medium.
Palate Barley-grain, nutty, clean, lingering on the tongue like a liqueur. Lots of depth.
Finish Full flavour. Malty sweetness develops to hints of Seville orange in a dryish finish.

SCORE 76

Other versions of Aberfeldy

Gordon and MacPhail's 1970 is being superseded by a '74. With a dash more sherry and wood, these are more intense and complex in perfume, but have a little less of the distillery character. The '74 bottling is marginally more malty. SCORE 75.

ABERLOUR

Distillery rating ☆☆☆☆   **Producer** Campbell Distillers
Region Highlands   **District** Speyside

LOVERS OF THE RICHER STYLE of Speyside malt rightly regard Aberlour as being in the top echelon. It is already complex and spicy (minty?) at 10 years old; there are odd sightings of a similar 12-year-old; and a 1964 version began a series of occasional vintage bottlings.

The village and distillery of Aberlour are in the heart of Speyside. The distillery probably pre-dates its first official recognition, in 1826. It was expanded in 1945, at its purchase by Campbell, now owned by Pernod Ricard. The whisky is made by Ian Mitchell, who was preceded in the job by his father and grandfather. The distillery is noted for its pristine cleanliness and fastidious attention to detail.

ABERLOUR 10-year-old, 40 vol
Colour Amber, with a reddish tinge.
Nose Full, malty, spicy, minty.
Body Remarkably soft and smooth. Medium to full.
Palate Distinctively clinging mouth-feel, with long-lasting flavour development. Dry, biscuity notes; malty sweetness; peppermint; spice (nutmeg?); and berry-fruit.
Finish Lingering, silky, flowery and clean.

SCORE 83

Other versions of Aberlour
A 1964 (43 vol) sampled was full of aroma, power and richness; exceptionally long, oaky finish. 1969 and '70 cask samples on the way there, but as yet more delicate. SCORE 88.

ARDBEG

Distillery rating ☆☆☆☆   **Producer** Allied Distillers
Region Islay   **District** South shore

THE EARTHY MALTS of Ardbeg are old-fashioned in the best sense of the phrase. Reminiscent of peat-smoke, burning grass, leafy bonfires, these are good, traditional, island whiskies. They are full of Islay character, yet their intensity quite overbalances them. The distillery may have its origins as far back as 1794. It was definitely operating by 1817. It is a fine example of a traditional malt distillery, and most handsome. After a short period of closure, it reopened in 1989, to the delight of enthusiasts for Islay malts. Its own maltings, which had a distinctive design, did not reopen. How will that affect future bottlings? Will the product retain its character to the full? There must be concern about that, but time will tell.

ARDBEG 10-year-old, 40 vol

Colour Fino sherry.
Nose Smoke, brine and iodine dryness.
Body Only medium to full, but very firm. A light-heavyweight with a punch worthy of a higher division.
Palate Skips sweetly along at first, then becomes mean and moody in the lengthy middle of the encounter.
Finish Hefty, lots of iodine.

SCORE 85

ARDBEG 15-year-old (distilled 1975, bottled 1990), 46 vol, Cadenhead

Colour Apricot.

Nose Iodine dryness in a complex with maltiness and sherry sweetness.

Body Medium, smooth, oily, firm.

Palate Malty-fruity, tasty, substantial, with sappy finish.

Finish Sappy, smoky, big, long.

SCORE 90

ARDBEG 1978, 40 vol, Gordon and MacPhail (cask sample)

Colour Reddish-amber, bright.

Nose Some iodine, but more fruity, sherryish notes.

Body Medium to full, oily, soft.

Palate Malty-fruity, perfumy, developing to delicate, leafy, smokiness.

Finish Lingering leafy smokiness and warmth.

SCORE 89

Other versions of Ardbeg

Two Signatory bottlings sampled. A 1972 at 59.6 vol was pale in colour; with a light, perfumy-malty nose; a very rich, syrupy, sweet body and palate; and an extremely, late, sudden, smokiness in the finish. Lacking in roundness and balance, but certainly interesting. SCORE 67.
A 1973 at 55.9 had the colour and aroma of Oloroso sherry; a medium to full body; and a sherryish palate, quickly combining with smoky dryness. SCORE 88. There have also been good bottlings from the Scotch Malt Whisky Society.

ARDMORE

Distillery rating ☆☆ **Producer** Allied Distillers
Region Highland **District** Speyside (Bogie)

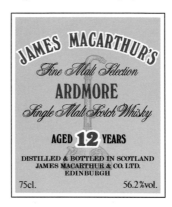

A PLEASANT, FAIRLY FULL, sweetish, whisky that is a component of the malty Teacher's blends. As a single malt, it is available only in independent bottlings. The distillery is on the eastern edge of Speyside, not far from Huntly, at Kennethmont between the river Bogie, the Clashindarroch Forest and the foothills of the Grampian mountains. Teacher's built this handsome distillery in 1898. Despite extensive expansions and modernisations in the 1950s and 1970s, it has preserved its steam engine and uses coal-fired stills.

ARDMORE 12-year-old, 56.2 vol, James MacArthur (cask sample)
Colour Full gold, bright.
Nose Fruity-sweet, malty, slightly spirity, powerful.
Body Soft, oily, drying in finish.
Palate Very sweet, malty, cedary, with some flowering currant.
Finish Softer, dry, with late burst of warmth.
SCORE 67

ARDMORE 1977, 59.4 vol, Gordon and MacPhail (cask sample)
Colour Very pale gold, almost white.
Nose Sweet, malty, spirity, powerful.
Body Full texture, clinging drily to the mouth.
Palate Malty, sweet, cedary, a hint of eucalyptus.
Finish Abrupt, powerful, warming.
SCORE 66

AUCHENTOSHAN

Distillery rating ☆☆☆☆☆   **Producer** Morrison Bowmore
Region Lowland   **District** West

CLASSIC STATUS has surely by now been earned by these definitively Lowland malts, made by the region's traditional triple-distillation method. They are very light, certainly, but that is the Lowland style. Nor does lightness mean lack of character. In their own quiet way, these are well-defined single malts, with plenty of complexity. If you fancy single malts, but do not care for intensity, Auchentoshan offers the perfect answer: subtlety. The name is pronounced "Och'n'tosh'n", as though it were an imprecation. The distillery is just outside Glasgow, on the city's northern fringes, hidden in a hollow between the river Clyde and the Kilpatrick Hills. It was founded around 1800, largely rebuilt after the Second World War and re-equipped in 1974. A decade later, it was acquired by a private company, Stanley P. Morrison, providing a Lowland partner for their excellent Islay and Highland distilleries, Bowmore and Glen Garioch. The company is now called Morrison Bowmore, and it produces a number of high-quality single malts in a variety of ages and versions.

AUCHENTOSHAN 10-year-old, 40 vol

Colour Pale gold.
Nose Clean and fresh, but also gentle. Delicate flowery-citrus note.
Body Soft.
Palate Lemon-grass notes. Lightly sweet without being sticky.
Finish Gingery and crisp.

SCORE 85

AUCHENTOSHAN 12-year-old, 40 vol, distillery sample

Colour Pale gold.

Nose A deft balance of freshness and maturity.

Body More rounded than the 10-year-old.

Palate The whisky world's reply to a good dry white vermouth?

Finish A bold note of linseed to flesh out the lemon-grass sweetness.

SCORE 86

AUCHENTOSHAN 18-year-old, 43 vol, distillery sample

Colour Fuller, old gold, colour.

Nose Fuller, hint of linseed, some sweetness.

Body More viscosity.

Palate For a light malt, a surprising depth.

Finish A hint of oakiness.

SCORE 86

AUCHENTOSHAN 1966, 43 vol

Colour Pale gold.

Nose Linseed again. Appetizing. A little drier.

Body Rounded but gentle. Oily.

Palate Starts sweet. Lots of flavour development. The sweetness seems to grow at first, then becomes spicy and flowery, drying with a hint of sherryish woodiness.

Finish Soothing, becoming firm, and eventually warming.

SCORE 86

AULTMORE

Distillery rating ☆☆☆   **Producer** United Distillers
Region Highland   **District** Speyside (Isla)

FINE MALT IN THE ROBUST, oaky style that seems to characterise the whiskies made near the river Isla. This distillery, just north of Keith, close to both the Isla and the Spey, was built in 1896 and reconstructed in 1971. The malt whisky is a component of Dewar's and the Robert Harvey blends. Bottlings of Aultmore single malt, subtitled "proprietors Robert Harvey and Co" have been in the market for some years. In 1991, the parent company, United Distillers, added a bottling with a label in their "flora and fauna" series. Both are at 12 years old, and similar, but the Robert Harvey bottlings seem drier. Aultmore is perhaps best before dinner, though not every taster agrees. Like one of the bigger fino sherries, it is both appetizing and relatively hefty. Perhaps it should be served with Scottish smoked-salmon *tapas*.

AULTMORE 12-year-old, 40 vol

Colour Very pale.
Nose Big bouquet, fresh, warm and drily perfumed.
Body Firm.
Palate Light and fruity, developing hints of gentian or quinine.
Finish Crisp, very dry.

SCORE 75

AULTMORE 12-year-old, 43 vol (cask sample)

Colour Very pale.

Nose Flowery, fresh, drily perfumed.

Body Medium, firm.

Palate Begins with a delicate, fruity-perfumy, sweetness, developing to a flowery dryness.

Finish Delicate, dry, extraordinarily appetizing.

SCORE 75

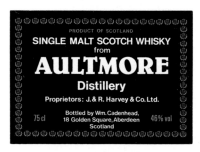

AULTMORE 13-year-old, 46 vol, Cadenhead (cask sample)

Colour Pale golden.

Nose Drier, with a hint of smoke.

Body Firm.

Palate Dry, flowery and expressive.

Finish Very dry.

SCORE 75

BALBLAIR

Distillery rating ☆☆☆   **Producer** Allied Distillers
Region Highlands   **District** Northern Highlands

T HE DRY SPICINESS of the Northern Highland malts manifests itself in definite but delicate form at Balblair. These are light-bodied, aromatic, whiskies best suited to being served before dinner. They are made from water that has flowed in streams over the crumbly local peat – hence the spiciness – and there is a Bourbon accent (albeit slight) in their maturation. This mountainous chunk of countryside plunges down from Ben Dearg (1,081m/3,547ft) by way of the Strathcarron river, to the Dornoch Firth and the sea. High on the Dornoch Firth, amid fields of sheep, and skirted by a single-track railway, is Balblair. Farther down the Firth, at nearby Tain, is Glenmorangie. Of the two, Balblair is older. Its roots go back to 1749, and the first distillery was built in 1790. The present building dates from the 1870s, and is little changed. The malt whisky is a component of the Ballantine's blends.

BALBLAIR Five-year-old, 40 vol
Balblair is regarded as a fast-maturing whisky, but the five-year-old might be just too youthful for some malt-lovers. Nonetheless, it has a good following in the important Italian market.

Colour	White wine.
Nose	Fresh, slightly sharp, and pear-like.
Body	Light
Palate	Clove-like spiciness.
Finish	Lingers, but not long enough.

SCORE 70

BALBLAIR 10-year-old, 40 vol

Colour Fuller than the five-year-old.

Nose The fruitiness has become softer and more fragrant.

Body More texture.

Palate Hints of tart, fresh raspberries, becoming sweeter.

Finish Much longer. Drys out to an olive-like finish.

SCORE 76

BALBLAIR 1964, 40 vol, Gordon and MacPhail

Colour Gold.

Nose More intense than the 10-year-old.

Body Light, smooth.

Palate More sweetness and intensity, with a dash of fino sherry.

Finish Very dry.

SCORE 76

BALBLAIR 1957, 40 vol, Gordon and MacPhail

Colour Gold.

Nose On the woody side, has dried out a lot.

Body Light, firm.

Palate Full, dry, with a spicy peatiness.

Finish Crisp.

SCORE 74

Set in its unspoiled pastoral setting in the Northern Highlands, Balblair is a pretty and unassuming distillery.

BALMENACH

Distillery rating ☆☆☆   **Producer** United Distillers
Region Highland   **District** Speyside

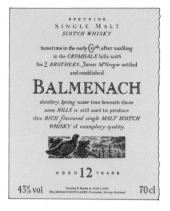

SPEYSIDE
SINGLE MALT
SCOTCH WHISKY

Sometime in the early 19th, after *walking*
in the *CROMDALE* hills *with*
his 2 *BROTHERS*, *James McGregor* settled
and established

BALMENACH

distillery. Spring water from beneath those
same HILLS is still used to produce
this *RICH flavoured single MALT SCOTCH*
WHISKY of *exemplary* quality.

AGED **12** YEARS

43% vol   Distilled & Bottled in SCOTLAND.   70cl
BALMENACH DISTILLERY, Cromdale, Moray, Scotland.

AN HISTORICALLY INTERESTING DISTILLERY in distant, mountain countryside between the upper reaches of the Spey and the Avon. Balmenach is amid a series of valleys called the Haughs of Cromdale. This area was well-known for the illicit production of whisky before distilling was legalised in the Highlands. The Balmenach distillery had a widespread reputation for its whisky before it became a legitimate operation in 1824, according to Sir Robert Bruce Lockhart, in his 1951 book *Scotch*. Balmenach is a component of many well-known blends, including Crabbie's, and had its first official bottling as a single malt in 1991.

BALMENACH 12-year-old, 43 vol (cask sample)
Colour Rich amber-red.
Nose Huge and deep. Pungent sherry character. Honeyish heather notes.
Body Medium to full. Soft and exceptionally smooth.
Palate Sherryish but dry. Alive with flavours: honey, ginger, bitter herbs, sappy, leafy notes.
Finish Rounded and satisfying.

SCORE 77

Other versions of Balmenach
Balmenach has the character to carry a lot of sherry ageing. This is a rare instance where the Gordon and MacPhail bottling (1971) is less sherried than the official version, but it is more flowery and smoky.
SCORE 71.

THE BALVENIE

Distillery rating ☆☆☆☆　　**Producer** William Grant & Sons
Region Highland　　**District** Speyside (Dufftown)

LUXURIOUS, HONEYISH, after-dinner malts from the distillery next door to Glenfiddich, in Dufftown. Both distilleries are owned by the same company, and always have been. Balvenie castle, designed by the Adam brothers in the 18th century, became the principal building of the Balvenie distillery when that was established in 1892. The whisky made at Balvenie is used primarily for blending, but in recent years it has been increasingly made available as a "super-premium" malt. Most of the single malt is matured in plain oak, but a substantial proportion goes into fino and sweet oloroso wood. The version called The Balvenie Founder's Reserve was originally vatted from distillates of between seven and 12-years-old, but now has a 10-year age statement. It is presented in a graceful bottle that looks set for the dinner table. The version called The Balvenie Classic has no age statement, but is at least 12-years-old. It spends its last year in sweet oloroso wood, and is presented in a slender, flask-shaped, bottle.

BALVENIE Founder's Reserve, 40 vol

Colour Amber.

Nose Faintly musky orange-honey perfume.

Body Medium.

Palate Sweet in taste, but slightly dry in texture. Lots of depth.

Finish Lingering, with just a touch of syrupiness.

SCORE 85

BALVENIE Classic, 43 vol

Colour Very full, amber, colour.

Nose Plenty of oloroso character.

Body Medium, rich.

Palate The sherry and the character of the Balvenie spirit dovetail impeccably.

Finish Long and warming.

SCORE 87

BALVENIE 15-year-old, 46 vol, Cadenhead (cask sample)

Colour Full gold.

Nose Powerful, dry, yet honeyish.

Body Medium.

Palate Orange-honey character, becoming drier.

Finish Big, round, full of fruity, flowery, honeyish, notes.

SCORE 80

BALVENIE 1974, 43 vol, Signatory

Colour Full gold.

Nose Flowery. Orange-honey.

Body Medium.

Palate Orange-honey character. Becoming drier still, but gentle. Lots of flavour development. Complex.

Finish Zest of orange peel.

SCORE 81

BANFF

Distillery rating ☆☆   **Producer** United Distillers
Region Highland   **District** Speyside (Deveron)

THE HOUSE OF COMMONS was once supplied with whisky from this small distillery. It was in the town whose name it bore, on the coast, west of the mouth of the river Deveron. The distillery, established in 1824, rebuilt on a different site in 1863, and again in 1877, and damaged by a bomb in the Second World War, was the subject of much folk history. None of this prevented it from being closed by its owners (then the Distillers Company Limited) in 1983 and dismantled. The whisky was used in the Slater, Rodger blends, and was never generally available as a single malt.

BANFF 1974, 40 vol, Gordon and MacPhail

Colour Full, golden.

Nose Pleasantly smoky aroma.

Body Medium.

Palate Clean, assertive and smoky-sweet.

Finish Clean, gingery.

SCORE 66

BEN NEVIS

Distillery rating ☆ **Producer** Ben Nevis Co.
Region Highland **District** Western Highlands

S COTLAND'S HIGHEST MOUNTAIN, Ben Nevis, (1344m/ 4409ft), gives its name to a distillery in the nearest town, Fort William. The distillery was established in 1825, by "Long John" McDonald, a 6ft 4in descendant of a ruler of the western Scottish kingdom of Argyll. He produced a whisky called Long John's Dew of Ben Nevis. The brand-name Long John eventually passed to another company, and is now owned by Allied. In 1989, the distillery was sold by Whitbread to Mitsui, partner of the Japanese whisky-makers Nikka. The new owners restored production of malt, but not grain, whisky in 1990, under the name Ben Nevis Distillery Co. Ltd. Dew of Ben Nevis is being reintroduced as a blend, but malts will be restricted to occasional single-cask bottlings until more stock has been produced. A 20-year-old sampled from the cask soon after the distillery reopened had a powerfully sherryish aroma; a firm body; a malty start, slightly toffeeish but becoming smoky, peaty and dry in a long finish. A much more impressive whisky than the very uneven independent bottlings.

BEN NEVIS 1966, 40 vol, Gordon and MacPhail

Colour Full, amber.

Nose Bourbon wood, vanilla and exotic fruits.

Body Oily and firm.

Palate Sweet and fruity.

Finish Sweet, almost meaty.

SCORE 55

PURE MALT SCOTCH WHISKY
from
BEN NEVIS
Distillery
Proprietors:
Ben Nevis Distillery (Fort William) Ltd.

Bottled by Wm. Cadenhead,
18 Golden Square, Aberdeen
Scotland

75 cl   46% vol

BEN NEVIS 22-year-old, 46 vol, Cadenhead (cask sample)

Colour Amber.

Nose Perfumy, Bourbon-like, slightly muddy.

Body Smooth.

Palate Caramel character.

Finish Big, quick.

$$\boxed{\text{SCORE 56}}$$

BEN NEVIS 1977, 62.4 vol, Scotch Malt Whisky Society

Colour Pale gold, bright.

Nose Nutty, oily, aromatic.

Body Full, smooth, lightly viscous, drying on tongue.

Palate More restrained fruitiness (mandarin?) in a sweet start, becoming drier and nutty.

Finish Very drying.

$$\boxed{\text{SCORE 61}}$$

BENRIACH

Distillery rating ☆☆☆   **Producer** Seagram
Region Highland   **District** Speyside (Lossie)

CONNOISSEURS
CHOICE

*Connoisseurs Choice, a
range of single malts from
various districts of
Scotland.*

*The distilleries situated in
the area of the valley of the
River Spey produce some of
the finest malt whiskies.*

SINGLE SPEYSIDE
MALT SCOTCH WHISKY
DISTILLED AT

BENRIACH
DISTILLERY
PROPRIETORS: The Longmorn-Glenlivet Distilleries Ltd

DISTILLED **1969** DISTILLED

SPECIALLY SELECTED PRODUCED AND BOTTLED BY
75cl   **GORDON & MACPHAIL**   40%vol
ELGIN · SCOTLAND
PRODUCT OF SCOTLAND

N EXT DOOR TO LONGMORN, and under the same
ownership. Both distilleries were built in the 1890s,
and extended in the 1960s and 70s. Longmorn has only
recently begun to market seriously its single malt (long
respected by those who had managed a sampling), and Benriach's is available only in independent bottlings. These will
change in year according to availability, and new vintages are
expected. Benriach has a floor maltings, and makes a good
Speyside whisky that is well worth sampling. It takes several
tastings to reveal the range of its subtlety and charm.

BENRIACH 1969, 40 vol, Gordon and MacPhail

Colour Gold.

Nose Flowering currant in the bouquet.

Body Light-to-medium.

Palate Firm and malty. On the dry side, but with hints of butterscotch.

Finish Dry, smoky, and warming in a vigorous, well-defined finish.

SCORE 69

BENRINNES

Distillery rating ☆☆☆   **Producer** United Distillers
Region Highlands   **District** Speyside

BEN RINNES (840m/2,759ft) is the dominant peak among the mountains overlooking the heart of Speyside. It gives its name, albeit rendered as one word, to a distillery at 213m (700ft). Benrinnes, which may have been founded as early as the 1820s, and certainly by the 1860s, was largely rebuilt in the 1950s. It had a long association with the Crawford blends. Its malt whisky, made by an unusual system of partially triple distillation, had its first official bottling in 1991.

BENRINNES 15-year-old, 43 vol

Colour	Autumnal reddish-brown.

Nose Heavy, almost creamy. A whiff of sherry, then a firm smoky "burnt toffee" character.

Body Medium to full. Firm.

Palate Dry, assertive, rounded. Flavours are gradually unlocked. Hints of licorice, aniseed, vanilla, bitter chocolate, smokiness.

Finish Satisfying, soothing. Faintly sweet, and smoky.

SCORE 79

BENRINNES 23-year-old, 46 vol, Cadenhead

Colour Pale gold.

Nose Very dry, fragrant.

Body Medium, smooth, rounded.

Palate Dry, malty, powerful.

Finish Dry, flowery, long.

SCORE 77

BENRINNES 1968, 40 vol, Gordon and MacPhail

Colour Amber.

Nose Deliciously fragrant, smoky.

Body Medium, very firm, smooth and well-rounded.

Palate Dry, gradually revealing a broad complex of interlocking flavours.

Finish Powerful, dry and smoky.

SCORE 78

BENROMACH

Distillery rating ☆☆☆   **Producer** United Distillers
Region Highland   **District** Speyside (Findhorn)

A DELICIOUS MALT, from a distillery that ceased production in 1983, and has since been partly dismantled. Benromach is at Forres, near the mouth of the Findhorn. The distillery was built in 1898 and, despite later refurbishment, seems eventually to have been regarded as too old and small to keep alive. As a single malt, its whisky is available only from independent bottlers. Gordon and MacPhail's 1968 is being superseded by the 1970.

BENROMACH 1970, 40 vol, Gordon and MacPhail (cask sample)
Colour Amber.
Nose Big, flowery, appetizing.
Body Medium to full, creamy.
Palate Malty, just lightly sweet but very clean and rounded; nutty, flowery, with a complex of delicate flavours.
Finish Full, smooth, satisfying, with a flicker of smoky dryness.

SCORE 78

Other versions of Benromach
The earlier, 1968, vintage was very similar, perhaps a fraction frutier and smokier, but less delicate in palate. SCORE 75.

BLADNOCH

Distillery rating ☆☆☆☆ **Producer** United Distillers
Region Lowland **District** Borders

CERTAINLY THE MOST SOUTHERLY of Scotland's distilleries. A definitively Lowland malt, too, in its grassy, lemony palate. The distillery stands far from any other, at Wigtown, by the river Bladnoch, on the Machars peninsula of Galloway. Despite its southern location, this is a somewhat isolated corner of Scotland, and it is rich in Celtic history. It saw the beginnings of Christianity in Scotland, and has associations with Robert the Bruce. The distillery was founded in the early 1800s, closed in 1938, reopened in the 1950s, and was taken over by Bells in 1983, not long before their acquisition by what is now United Distillers.

BLADNOCH Eight-year-old, 40 vol
Light it may be, but very distinctive. Also very enjoyable.
A delicious desert malt (perhaps with creme brulée?)

Colour	Pale yellow.

Nose Grassy, lemony character right from the start.

Body Very light, but firm.

Palate At first seems delicate in flavour, but this develops and becomes surprisingly full.

Finish The citrus character emerges quite strongly in the finish which is remarkably big for a light Lowland malt.

SCORE 85

LOWLAND
SINGLE MALT
SCOTCH WHISKY

The *Broad Leaved Helleborine*,
a rare species of *wild orchid*, can be found growing
in the *ancient oak woodland* behind the

BLADNOCH

distillery. The most southerly in *SCOTLAND*,
founded in the *early 1800's*. 𝒜 the
distillery stands by the *RIVER BLADNOCH*
near *Wigtown*. It produces a *distinctive*
LOWLAND single MALT WHISKY ~ delicate and
fruity with a *lemony* aroma and *taste*.

A G E D **10** Y E A R S

43% vol   70 cl

BLADNOCH 10-year-old, 43 vol (cask sample)

Colour Amber.

Nose Hint of sherry, fragrantly fruity, lemony.

Body Fuller, firm.

Palate Lots of development, from a sherryish start through cereal-grain grassiness to flowery, fruity, lemony notes.

Finish Again, suprisingly big, and long-lasting.

SCORE 85

BLADNOCH 1975, 40 vol, Gordon and MacPhail

Colour Fuller than the eight-year-old.

Nose Hint of sherry.

Body Soft, quite luscious.

Palate Still that lemony character.

Finish A bigger finish.

SCORE 86

BLADNOCH 1966, 43 vol, Signatory

Colour Full gold.

Nose Very flowery.

Body Very firm.

Palate Flowery, lemony, some sweet maltiness.

Finish Lemony, slightly tart, appetizing, long.

SCORE 85

BLAIR ATHOL

Distillery rating ☆☆☆   **Producer** United Distillers
Region Highlands   **District** Midlands

THE VILLAGE SPELLS ATHOLL with the double "l" while the distillery prefers to stay single. Village and distillery are on the whisky route between Speyside and the blending and shipping town of Perth. The mountain resort of Pitlochry, known for its summer theatre, is not far away. The distillery traces its origins to 1798, and was most recently extended in the 1970s.

BLAIR ATHOL Eight-year-old, 40 vol
Colour Pale gold.
Nose Fresh and very clean. A suggestion of ginger, or shortbread.
Body Light to medium.
Palate Dryish start. Aromatic. Hints of butterscotch and ginger.
Finish A little more gingery in its smooth, round finish.

SCORE 75

BLAIR ATHOL 12-year-old, 43 vol (cask sample)
Colour Bronze.
Nose Still very fresh, some sherry, ginger, shortbread.
Body Medium.
Palate Sherry, shortbread, ginger, fruity dryness.
Finish Smooth, round, warming.

SCORE 76

BOWMORE

Distillery rating ☆☆☆☆   **Producer** Morrison Bowmore
Region Islay   **District** Loch Indaal

O NE OF THE GREAT MALT DISTILLERIES, in the village
of Bowmore, "capital" of Islay. The village is in the
middle of the island, on the inlet called Loch Indaal.
The distillery's production is equidistant from the most intense
malts of the south shore and the gentlest extreme of the north.
Its single malts match Islay's geography, providing a balance
between Islay character at its most intense and at its most
subtle. This balance is not a compromise; it is an enigma.
Tasters have found it infuriatingly difficult to unravel that
enigma. One taster detected a lavender character. That might
be one strand. Lavender, heather, honey, and flowering currant
have all been noticed by tasters. These are complex malts with
their own distinct character, and great finesse. Delightful after-
dinner malts. The water rises from peat and flows by way of the
river Laggan over the same magic earth for about eight miles to
the distillery. The company has its own maltings, and uses a
fairly gentle technique of peating there. The maturation warehouses are doused with four or five feet of water at high tide,
but this shore is less exposed than the south. All of these
factors, and a great deal of care at a model distillery, create the
Bowmore character. The distillery is Morrison's "flagship".

*In this copper-domed mash tun, the barley malted at Bowmore and the
island's peaty water meet and infuse on the way to becoming whisky.*

BOWMORE 10-year-old, 40 vol

Colour Amber, fuller than previous bottlings at this age.

Nose Hint of sherry. Light saltiness. Spicy aromas. Lavender. Heather.

Body Light to medium.

Palate Lightly sweet, then spicy and heathery. Hint of smoke.

Finish Appetizing. Lingering, late, saltiness. A delightful aperitif.

SCORE 82

BOWMORE 12-year-old, 43 vol

Colour Amber. Again, slightly fuller than before.

Nose More salt, seaweed and smoke than at 10 years.

Body Medium. Lightly syrupy.

Palate Persistent sherry sweetness. Spicy, heathery, seaweedy, salty. Complex, with lots of flavour development.

Finish Remarkably long and salty.

SCORE 87

BOWMORE Bicentenary (15-year-old, but no age statement), 43 vol

Colour Amber.

Nose Lots of flowering currant (a little too much for balance?).

Body Slightly oily.

Palate More sherry character. Heathery, seaweedy.

Finish Very long.

SCORE 87

BOWMORE 21-year-old, 43 vol (cask sample)

Colour Full gold to amber.

Nose Hugely aromatic. Sherry, oak, smoke, heather,
and especially seaweed.

Body Medium to full, rich.

Palate Sherry, marzipan, nuts, oiliness, seaweed, salt.
Astonishingly complex.

Finish Heathery, aromatic, characteristically long, warming.

SCORE 89

BOWMORE 25-year-old, 43 vol (cask sample)

Colour Deep amber-red.

Nose Sherry, powerful lavender and heather. Powerfully fragrant.

Body Medium to full, drying on tongue.

Palate Hefty sherry. Gradual emergence of oak, smoke, heather,
lavender, seaweed and salt.

Finish Sappy, smoky, salty, warming.

SCORE 88

BRACKLA

Distillery rating ☆☆☆   **Producer** United Distillers
Region Highlands   **District** Speyside (Findhorn Valley)

MAJESTIC MALT. The distillery lies between the river Findhorn and the Moray Firth, at Cawdor, not far from Nairn. It was founded in 1812, and permitted to style itself Royal Brackla in 1835, because King William IV enjoyed the whisky. Royal Brackla was rebuilt in 1898 and again in 1966, and extended in 1970. It closed in 1985 but reopened in 1991. Its whisky has been an important component of the Bisset blends. As a single malt, it is available only from independents, but there could be an official bottling in the future.

CONNOISSEURS CHOICE

Connoisseurs Choice, a range of single malts from various districts of Scotland.

In the Highlands are situated the greatest number of malt whisky distilleries.

SINGLE HIGHLAND
MALT SCOTCH WHISKY
DISTILLED AT
ROYAL BRACKLA
DISTILLERY
PROPRIETORS: John Bisset & Co. Ltd
DISTILLED **1970** DISTILLED
SPECIALLY SELECTED, PRODUCED AND BOTTLED BY
75cl   GORDON & MACPHAIL   40%vol
ELGIN · SCOTLAND
PRODUCT OF SCOTLAND

ROYAL BRACKLA 1970, 40 vol, Gordon and MacPhail
Despite its powerful sweetness, a perilously drinkable after-dinner malt. It also has a wonderful balance of peat-smoke and malt, the classic ingredients.

Colour Old gold.

Nose Big, smoky aroma, with malty notes – almost a hint of molasses.

Body Medium to full.

Palate Extraordinarily smooth, malty and chewy. Develops an intense sweetness, becoming fruity (raisiny?) and perfumy.

Finish Very dry, with a cedary, "cigar box" character.

SCORE 77

PRODUCT OF SCOTLAND
SINGLE MALT SCOTCH WHISKY
from
ROYAL BRACKLA
Distillery
Proprietors: J. Bisset & Co. Ltd.
Bottled by Wm. Cadenhead,
75 cl   18 Golden Square, Aberdeen   46% vol
Scotland

ROYAL BRACKLA 23-year-old, 46 vol, Cadenhead (cask sample)

Colour Bright gold.

Nose Malty, sweetish, with some smokiness at the back of the nose.

Body Soft at first, becoming slightly dry on the tongue.

Palate Sweetish, perfumy.

Finish Dry, warming, very long.

SCORE 76

BRUICHLADDICH

Distillery rating ☆☆☆   **Producer** Invergordon
Region Islay   **District** Loch Indaal

A GOOD SINGLE MALT for the newcomer to Islay. Bruichladdich is on the north shore of Loch Indaal, facing Bowmore across the water. Bruichladdich's water rises from a hillside spring, and flows over peat. It is, however, a less peaty water than some used by other distilleries. Bruichladdich's stills have tall necks, producing a relatively light, clean spirit. Unlike the other Islay distilleries, it is separated from the sea, albeit only by a quiet coast road, across which it has an old loading pier. It was founded in 1881, rebuilt in 1886, and – despite an extension in 1975 – little changed since. Bruichladdich is now the most westerly working distillery in Scotland.

PRODUCT OF SCOTLAND

BRUICHLADDICH

ISLAY

AGED 10 YEARS

SINGLE MALT
SCOTCH WHISKY

DISTILLED AND BOTTLED BY
BRUICHLADDICH DISTILLERY CO.LTD.
BRUICHLADDICH ISLE OF ISLAY

Founded 1881

BRUICHLADDICH 10-year-old, 40 vol
This deceptive malt's dimensions become more evident at older ages, but thus far these have been available only in the odd bottling. The other distillers on Islay rate Bruichladdich highly.

Colour Pale.	
Nose Hint of seaweed.	
Body Light, but smooth and firm.	
Palate Clean, crisp and dry at first, with hints of peat, becoming quite sweet as it evolves.	
Finish Deceptive; seeming at first simply delicate, but gradually revealing a wider range of subtleties.	

SCORE 76

PRODUCT OF SCOTLAND

BRUICHLADDICH

ISLAY

AGED 15 YEARS
SINGLE MALT
SCOTCH WHISKY

DISTILLED AND BOTTLED BY
BRUICHLADDICH DISTILLERY CO.LTD.
BRUICHLADDICH ISLE OF ISLAY

Founded 1881

75cl   Bottled in Scotland   43%vol

BRUICHLADDICH 15-year-old, 43 vol

Colour Old gold.

Nose Hint of sea. Seaweed, grass, malt.

Body Light to medium. Firm. Lightly oily. Smooth.

Palate More assertive. Notes of saltiness, grassy maltiness and flowery peatiness. Complex interplay of elements.

Finish Again, that crisp, grassy, maltiness, with some sweetness. Long, gentle. A malt upon (and with) which to reflect at length.

SCORE 78

BRUICHLADDICH 19-year-old, 46 vol, Cadenhead (cask sample)

Colour Full gold.

Nose Full, with hints of seaweed, and some sweetness.

Body Light to medium, smooth.

Palate Hint of clean sweetness at first, quickly developing to lightly peaty, seaweedy, salty notes.

Finish Big, smooth, delicious.

SCORE 79

BRUICHLADDICH 25-year-old, 46 vol, Cadenhead (cask sample)

Colour Pale.

Nose Hints of seaweed, and some woodiness.

Body Light to medium, very smooth.

Palate Sweet, hints of seaweed, some woodiness. Hint of sulphur.

Finish Aromatic, dry.

SCORE 74

BUNNAHABHAIN

Distillery rating ☆☆☆ **Producer** Highland Distilleries
Region Islay **District** North shore

S OMETIMES DESCRIBED AS BEING the Islay malt that lacks the island character. That is to misunderstand this delicious whisky. Among the Islay malts, Bunnahabhain is the lightest in palate, but its body has a distinctive oiliness. Bunnahabhain does have a faint, flowery, nutty hint of peatiness, and a whiff of sea-air, in a character that is quietly distinctive. The distillery, established in 1881, is set round a courtyard in a style that resembles a chateau in Bordeaux. Despite expansion in 1963, the distillery is little changed. Its water comes from streams in the hills, but is piped, and therefore less peaty than might otherwise be expected. The stills are large, in the style that the industry calls onion-shaped, though in this instance, pear-shaped might be a better description. Bunnahabhain emphasises the narrowness of the cut taken from the stills. A proportion of sherry is used in maturation. A 1964 vintage from Signatory is more intense, and maltier than the official version.

BUNNAHABHAIN 12-year-old, 40 vol
Colour Gold.
Nose Remarkably fresh "sea air" aroma.
Body Light to medium, firm.
Palate Gentle, clean, nutty-malty sweetness.
Finish Very full flavour development. A refreshing quality.

SCORE 77

CAOL ILA

Distillery rating ☆☆☆☆ **Producer** United Distillers
Region Islay **District** North shore

L ONG ENJOYED BY DEVOTEES for its Islay character, distinctive spiciness, and surprising drinkability. For years, it could be found only as an independent bottling, but Caol Ila went on sale in an "official" version in 1988/9. With its limited availability and its difficult name (pronounced "cull-eela"), it has been almost a secret Islay malt. The Gaelic word Caol is in English "kyle", meaning "sound", as in a narrow strip of water. Caol Ila means "Sound of Islay". The distillery, appropriately hidden, is in a cove near Port Askaig, overlooking the Sound of Islay, across which the ferry chugs to the nearby island of Jura. The water source for Caol Ila is a peaty loch about a mile away, from which the water flows through fields. The stills are large, and lantern shaped. Caol Ila was built in 1846, reconstructed in 1879, and rather brusquely modernised in the 1970s. Its whisky has been a component of a vatted malt called Glen Ila, and the Bulloch and Lade blends. As a single malt, Caol Ila is a lively whisky, peaty and full of flavour without being as intense as its more famous counterparts.

CAOL ILA 12-year-old, 40 vol

Colour Pale, "white wine".
Nose Peaty, seaweedy, fruity.
Body Light, but very firm, becoming slightly syrupy.
Palate Peaty, peppery, spicy, olive-like.
Finish Peppery, warming.

SCORE 77

CAOL ILA 12-year-old, 65.5 vol, Cadenhead

Colour Fino sherry.

Nose Very slightly drier and less oily.

Body Light, firm, smooth.

Palate Very slightly sweeter, with more malt. Slightly spirity.

Finish Very warming.

SCORE 77

ISLAY
SINGLE MALT *SCOTCH WHISKY*

CAOL ILA

distillery, built in 1846 is situated near *Port Askaig* on the *Isle of Islay.* Steamers used to call twice a week to collect *whisky* from this remote *site* in a cove facing the *Isle of Jura.* Water supplies for mashing come from *Loch nam Ban* although the sea provides *water for condensing.* Unusual for an *Islay* this *single MALT SCOTCH WHISKY* has *a fresh aroma* and a *light yet well rounded* flavour.

AGED **15** YEARS

43% vol Distilled & Bottled in *SCOTLAND.* CAOL ILA DISTILLERY Port Askaig, Isle of Islay, Scotland. 70 cl

CAOL ILA 15-year-old, 43 vol (cask sample)

Colour Fino sherry. Bright.

Nose Aromatic, complex.

Body Light, very firm, smooth.

Palate Rounder, with the flavours more combined.

Finish Oily and warming enough to keep out the sea.

SCORE 80

CAOL ILA 1977, 40 vol, Gordon and MacPhail (cask sample)

Colour Amber.

Nose Interesting blend of sherry, peat and assertive sea.

Body Light to medium. Smooth.

Palate The sherry seems to bring out more malty sweetness.

Finish Smooth, warming.

SCORE 77

Other versions of Caol Ila

A 12-year-old (63.7 vol) James MacArthur bottling was smooth and oily, with some malty sweetness. SCORE 78. A Scotch Malt Whisky Society bottling, 1978 and 65.3 vol, was pale, malty and relatively mild. SCORE 77.

CAPERDONICH

Distillery rating ☆☆☆   **Producer** Seagram
Region Highlands   **District** Speyside (Rothes)

PARTNER TO THE RENOWNED Glen Grant. The two distilleries, under the same ownership, are across the street from one another, in the whisky town of Rothes. This little town, on the Spey, has five distilleries. Caperdonich, founded in 1898, was rebuilt in 1965 and extended in 1967. From the start, it has been Number Two to Glen Grant. The malts of both distilleries are light and fragrant in their bouquet, medium-bodied, and nutty-tasting. Of the two, Caperdonich is perhaps a dash fruitier, and slightly more smoky. The malts of both distilleries are components of Chivas Regal, and of many other blends. As a single malt, it is available only in independent bottlings.

CAPERDONICH 1968, 40 vol, Gordon and MacPhail
The lesser known Speyside malts can still have plenty of style, and this is a good example.

Colour Full, golden.

Nose Fragrant, smoky.

Body Light to medium, dryish.

Palate Malty, nutty and fruity. A hint of coconut?

Finish Seems at first abrupt, but turns out to be lingering, warming and slightly smoky.

SCORE 73

CAPERDONICH 23-year-old, 46 vol, Cadenhead (cask sample)

Colour Very full gold.

Nose Very smoky, fragrant. Superb.

Body Medium, softer.

Palate Delicious. Coconut character, without being sweet.
Lots of depth and complexity.

Finish Smooth and long. A lovely after-dinner malt.

SCORE 75

CARDHU

Distillery rating ☆☆☆   **Producer** United Distillers
Region Highlands   **District** Speyside

AN EASY INTRODUCTION to single malts. A light-tasting, sweetish malt that is clearly seen by its producers as a natural competitor with Glendfiddich. Having made a later entry to the market as a single malt, Cardhu is now becoming very widely available worldwide. It is also, and has been for many years, part of the malty "middle" of the Johnnie Walker blends (the more distinct top notes of Johnnie Walker are from Talisker). Cardhu has in the past been variously known as Cardow and Cardoor. These spellings all refer to the same hamlet, in the heart of Speyside, on the stretch of the river known as Knockando. The same stretch houses the unrelated Knockando and Tamdhu distilleries. It is also a favoured spot for salmon fishermen. The Cardhu distillery traces its history to 1824, and on the present site to 1884. It was extended in 1887 and 1897, and rebuilt in 1961.

CARDHU 12-year-old, 40 vol
Colour Pale.
Nose Light, appetizing, with faint hint of smoke.
Body Light and smooth.
Palate Light to medium in flavour, with the emphasis on malty sweetness.
Finish A lingering, syrupy sweetness, but also a rounder dryness with late hints of peat, though again faint.

SCORE 72

CLYNELISH

Distillery rating ☆☆☆☆   **Producer** United Distillers
Region Highlands   **District** Northern Highlands

HIGHLAND
SINGLE MALT
SCOTCH WHISKY

One of the most *northerly* in *Scotland.*

CLYNELISH

distillery, was established in *Brora*
by the *Marquess* of *STAFFORD*
in 1819. Its building *signalled* the
end of illicit *distilling*
in the area and provided a
ready market for locally grown
barley. Water is piped from the
CLYNEMILTON burn to produce this
fruity, & slightly smoky single
MALT SCOTCH WHISKY much
appreciated by *connoisseurs.*

YEARS **14** OLD

43% vol   70cl

Distilled & Bottled in *SCOTLAND,*
CLYNELISH DISTILLERY
Brora, Sutherland, Scotland

A CLASSIC CASE of a coastal malt having a slightly "island" character. The location helps, and medium-peated malt is used. Clynelish is at the fishing and golfing resort of Brora. The original Clynelish distillery was founded in 1819 by the first Duke of Sutherland, and closed in the 1980s. The present distillery opened in 1967. A 12-year-old, at 40 vol, is being replaced by a less sherryish 14, at 43 vol.

CLYNELISH 14-year-old, 43 vol

Colour Pale gold.

Nose Sea, perhaps seaweed, and peat.

Body Medium to full, smooth. Visibly oily.

Palate Starts malty (sweetish when water is added), becoming fruity-spicy (mustard?), with notes of seaweed and salt.

Finish Remarkable lingering spiciness. Stays very fresh, with an emphatic mustard flavour. Reminiscent of mustard-cress. A tremendously appetizing malt.

SCORE 81

COLEBURN

Distillery rating ☆☆   **Producer** United Distillers
Region Highlands   **District** Speyside (Lossie)

CONNOISSEURS CHOICE

Connoisseurs Choice, a range of single malts from various districts of Scotland.

The distilleries situated in the area of the valley of the River Spey produce some of the finest malt whiskies.

SINGLE SPEYSIDE
MALT SCOTCH WHISKY
DISTILLED AT

COLEBURN
DISTILLERY
PROPRIETORS: J. & G. Stewart Ltd

DISTILLED 1972 DISTILLED

SPECIALLY SELECTED, PRODUCED AND BOTTLED BY
75cl   GORDON & MACPHAIL   40%vol
ELGIN · SCOTLAND
PRODUCT OF SCOTLAND

A LIGHT, FLOWERY, FIRM, LIVELY, pre-dinner malt that has traditionally been a component of the Andrew Usher blended whiskies. As a single malt, Coleburn can be found only in independent bottlings. The distillery, which is very small, is on the east of the river Lossie, between the towns of Elgin and Rothes. It was built in 1896, and has been temporarily closed since 1985.

COLEBURN 1972, 40 vol, Gordon and MacPhail (cask sample)
Colour Fuller gold.
Nose Sweetness and dryness, with a hint of smoke.
Body Light but firm.
Palate Slightly oily, cereal-grain, sweetness. Becoming drier and faintly smoky.
Finish Still oily-sweet, becoming dry, warming. Falls away somewhat.

SCORE 66

CONVALMORE

Distillery rating ☆☆   **Producer** United Distillers
Region Highlands   **District** Speyside (Dufftown)

CHEEK-BY-JOWL with Glenfiddich and Balvenie, in Dufftown, but not a member of their family. Convalmore's malt has traditionally been a component of the Lowries blended whiskies, among others. As a single, a biggish, after-dinner malt, it is available only in independent bottlings. The distillery was founded in 1894, rebuilt in 1910, and extended in 1964. It has been temporarily closed since 1985.

CONVALMORE 1969, 40 vol, Gordon and MacPhail
An unassuming, enjoyable digestif.

Colour Full, gold.	

Colour Full, gold.

Nose Very pleasant, sweetish.

Body Medium to full.

Palate Smooth, slightly syrupy texture. Sweet, but not at all cloying, at first. Develops towards malty dryness.

Finish Hints of ginger, spiciness and peat in an aromatic, dry finish.

SCORE 68

CRAGGANMORE

Distillery rating ☆☆☆☆ **Producer** United Distillers
Region Highlands **District** Speyside

O NE OF THE GREAT Speyside malts, but far less widely known than might be expected. Its austere, haughty, style means that it will always be a malt for the serious devotee. Nor will it ever come into great supply, as the distillery is quite small. Cragganmore has, however, become a little more widely available since it was launched in an "official" bottling, at 12-years-old, in 1988/9, as part of the Classic Malts range assembled by United Distillers. In that range, each malt represents a different district. Cragganmore is the Speyside choice. The malt is also available in independent bottlings. Cragganmore malt has traditionally been a component of the Old Parr blended whiskies, which are especially popular in Japan. The distillery, once part owned by the Ballindalloch Estate, is high on the Spey, where the river meets the Avon and Livet. Cragganmore was founded in 1869, rebuilt in 1902, and extended in 1964.

CRAGGANMORE 12-year-old, 40 vol

Colour Golden.

Nose The most complex aroma of any malt. Its bouquet is astonishingly fragrant and delicate with sweetish notes of cut grass and herbs (thyme perhaps?).

Body Light to medium, but very firm and smooth.

Palate Delicate, clean, restrained, with a huge range of herbal flowery notes.

Finish Long.

SCORE 90

CRAGGANMORE 1974, 40 vol, Gordon and MacPhail

Colour Slightly fuller than the 1972 version.

Nose Slightly softer. Fragrant, with light peat-smoke.

Body Full but soft.

Palate Astonishingly perfumy and spicy. More complex.

Finish Gentler but very long.

SCORE 88

CRAGGANMORE 1972, 40 vol, Gordon and MacPhail
Lacks the aloofness and mystery of the official version, but a
splendidly rounded, complex malt in its own right.

Colour Golden.

Nose A new peat-smoke accent.

Body Fuller.

Palate More pronounced sweetness, followed by an assertive
development of flavour.

Finish Much more powerful.

SCORE 85

CRAIGELLACHIE

Distillery rating ☆☆☆   **Producer** United Distillers
Region Highlands   **District** Speyside

W HERE THE FIDDICH meets the Spey, and the district's main roads cross, between Dufftown, Aberlour and Rothes, the village of Craigellachie has a bridge designed by the great Scottish engineer Thomas Telford, a cooperage, and two distilleries. The one called simply Craigellachie stands to the south-east of the Spey. To the north-west is Macallan. Craigellachie is pronounced "Craig-ella-ki". The last "i" is short. Its full-flavoured, malty-fruity whisky is a component of the White Horse blends. As a single malt, it is now available in the "flora and fauna" series by United Distillers. The distillery was founded in 1891, and rebuilt in a modern style in 1965.

CRAIGELLACHIE 14-year-old, 43 vol (cask sample)
Colour Old gold.
Nose Fragrant. Lightly smoky. Plenty of sweet, crushed-barley maltiness.
Body Medium.
Palate Starts sweet, slightly syrupy, and malty; becomes nutty; then develops a very fruity, Seville orange character.
Finish Orangey, lightly smoky, aromatic, warming.

SCORE 75

CRAIGELLACHIE 1974, 40 vol, Gordon and MacPhail

Colour Amber.

Nose More emphatic and complex in its fragrance.

Body Medium.

Palate Softer. Nutty. Falls away somewhat.

Finish Lightly smoky, gently warming.

SCORE 73

PURE MALT SCOTCH WHISKY
from
Craigellachie-Glenlivet
Distillery

Proprietors : White Horse Distillers Ltd.

75 cl   Bottled by Wm.Cadenhead,
18 Golden Square, Aberdeen   46% vol
Scotland

CRAIGELLACHIE 26-year-old, 46 vol, Cadenhead (cask sample)

Colour Pale, "white wine".

Nose Fragrant, dry.

Body Very soft and smooth.

Palate Minty and malty, sweetish. Distinctive and enjoyable.

Finish Minty, rather quick.

SCORE 72

DAILUAINE

Distillery rating ☆☆☆ **Producer** United Distillers
Region Highlands **District** Speyside

BETWEEN THE MOUNTAIN Ben Rinnes and the river Spey, at the hamlet of Carron, not far from Aberlour, the Dailuaine ("Dal-oo-ayn") distillery produces a robust, tasty, after-dinner malt that is a component of the Johnnie Walker blended whiskies, among others. It is now available as a single malt in United Distillers' "flora and fauna" series. The distillery was founded in 1852, and has been rebuilt several times, most recently in 1960. It is one of several distilleries along the Spey valley that had their own railway halts, for workers and visitors – and as a means of shipping in barley or malt and despatching whisky. Although the railway line has now been removed, the route has been preserved for walkers as the "Speyside Way", from Tomintoul to the sea. Dailuaine had its own steam locomotive, which is preserved on the Strathspey Railway at Aviemore.

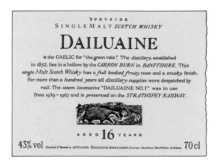

SPEYSIDE
SINGLE MALT *SCOTCH WHISKY*

DAILUAINE

is the GAELIC for "the green vale". The *distillery*, established in 1852, lies in a hollow by the *CARRON BURN* in *BANFFSHIRE*. This *single Malt Scotch Whisky* has a *full bodied fruity* nose and a *smoky* finish. For more than a *hundred years* all *distillery supplies* were despatched by *rail*. The *steam locomotive* "DAILUAINE NO.1" was in use from 1939 – 1967 and is *preserved* on the *STRATHSPEY RAILWAY*.

AGED **16** YEARS

43% vol Distilled & Bottled in SCOTLAND. DAILUAINE DISTILLERY. Carron. Aberlour. Banffshire. Scotland. 70 cl

DAILUANE 16-year-old, 43 vol (cask sample)

Colour Emphatically reddish amber.

Nose Sherryish but dry, perfumy.

Body Medium to full, smooth.

Palate Sherryish, with "barley sugar" maltiness, but always balanced by a dry, cedar or oak, background.

Finish Sherryish, smooth, very warming, long.

SCORE 76

CONNOISSEURS CHOICE

Connoisseurs Choice, a range of single malts from various districts of Scotland.

The distilleries situated in the area of the valley of the River Spey produce some of the finest malt whiskies.

SINGLE SPEYSIDE MALT SCOTCH WHISKY
DISTILLED AT
DAILUAINE
DISTILLERY
PROPRIETORS: Dailuaine-Talisker Distilleries Ltd
DISTILLED 1971 DISTILLED

SPECIALLY SELECTED PRODUCED AND BOTTLED BY
75cl   **GORDON & MACPHAIL**   40%vol
ELGIN · SCOTLAND
PRODUCT OF SCOTLAND

DAILUAINE 1971, 40 vol, Gordon and MacPhail

Colour Gold.

Nose Fragrant, long-lasting, beginning dry, with malty notes, and a suggestion of sherry, gradually becoming sweeter.

Body Medium to full, quite fleshy.

Palate Restrained sweetness, some syrupy maltiness and a dash of fruit.

Finish Oaky.

SCORE 74

DAILUAINE 22-year-old, 46 vol, Cadenhead (cask sample)

Colour Very pale, "white wine".

Nose Fragrant, on the dry side, but also with some sweet notes.

Body Medium to full, soft.

Palate Sweet, fruity, aromatic.

Finish Soft, fruity, aromatic. A 23-year-old version is perhaps marginally drier.

SCORE 73

Other versions of Dailuaine
A Scotch Malt Whisky Society bottling, 1975 and 57.3 vol, had a greenish hue, a smokier nose, but a sweeter palate. Not so much barley sugar as toffee. SCORE 72.

DALLAS DHU

Distillery rating ☆☆☆☆   **Producer** United Distillers
Region Highlands   **District** Speyside (Findhorn)

RESERVED FOR POSTERITY as a traditional and historic distillery, but no longer producing its delicious, rich, malt. Dallas Dhu, founded in 1899, and little changed, closed in the early 1980s and reopened its doors to the public in 1988 under the aegis of Scotland's Historic Buildings and Monument Directorate. There are no plans to restart production. The distillery is between the rivers Findhorn and Lossie, and five or six miles west of the village of Dallas. The name Dallas derives from the Gaelic words for valley and water. Dhu means black, or perhaps in this instance "dark". It is not certain whether this refers to the colour of the water or the valley, or derives from an earlier brand name for a blended whisky made with the Dallas malt. The malt has been bottled as a single in recent years by Gordon and MacPhail. They no longer have supplies. There may be the odd cask somewhere in Scotland, and bottles still linger in a few lucky shops and bars.

DALLAS DHU 1971, 40 vol, Gordon and MacPhail
Colour Full, amber.
Nose Complex, with some peaty, flowery sweetness, malt and oak.
Body Full, sweetly clinging and liqueurish. Almost chewy.
Palate Malt, dark chocolate, and a dash of bitter, leafy smokiness.
Finish Smooth, oak-sappy, dry, long.

SCORE 85

DALMORE

Distillery rating ☆☆☆☆   **Producer** Whyte and Mackay
Region Highlands   **District** Northern Highlands

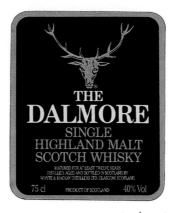

NOBLE, AFTER-DINNER MALT that is not as widely appreciated as it might be. Once owned by a distinguished local family, the Mackenzies', whose friends James Whyte and Charles Mackay created a famous name in blended Scotch. A Mackenzie managed the distillery until the late 1980s. Whyte and Mackay is now owned by American Brands, whose other interests include Jim Beam. The Dalmore distillery, said to have been founded in 1839, bears a passing resemblance to a country railway station. Its offices are partly panelled with carved oak that once graced a shooting lodge. Much of the malt is aged in sherry casks. A 30-year-old limited edition in 1989 was sherryish, nutty, and silky-smooth, with no hint of woodiness.

DALMORE 12-year-old, 40 vol

Colour Full, amber.

Nose Powerful, with sherry, fruit and malt.

Body Medium to full, but never very sweet or sticky. Soft.

Palate Rounded and velvet-smooth, with a big development of dry, spicy, bitter-sweet marmalade-like orange and heathery, smoky flavours. Even a faint tang of saltiness.

Finish Long, with more orangey notes.

SCORE 79

DALWHINNIE

Distillery rating ☆☆☆ **Producer** United Distillers
Region Highlands **District** Speyside

THE HIGHEST DISTILLERY in Scotland, at 326m (1,073ft). It is still in a glen, with the Monadhlaith Mountains to one side, the Forest of Atholl, the Cairngorms and the Grampians to the other. Dalwhinnie is Gaelic for "meeting place", and the village of this name stands at the junction of old cattle-droving routes from the west and north down to the Central Lowlands. Much whisky smuggling went on along this route. Running in front of the distillery is the river Truim, one of several that feed the Spey. The Dalwhinnie distillery was called Strathspey when it opened in 1897. Stretching a point, it can regard itself as being on Speyside, though it is 25 miles or more from the beginning of the dense distillery country to the north. Dalwhinnie was damaged by fire in 1934 and reopened in 1938. Its malt whisky has traditionally been an important component of the Buchanan blends, and it represents The Highlands in United Distillers' Classic Malts ranges. The distillery also serves as a meteorological observation post.

DALWHINNIE 15-year-old, 43 vol
Colour Gold.
Nose Very aromatic; dry, faintly phenolic, lightly peaty.
Body Firm, slightly oily.
Palate Remarkably smooth, long lasting flavour development. Aromatic, heather-honey notes give way to cut-grass, malty sweetness, which intensifies until a sudden burst of peat.
Finish Very long.

SCORE 76

DALWHINNIE 1970, 40 vol, Gordon and MacPhail

Colour Slightly fuller.

Nose More phenol, more emphatic peatiness.

Body Fuller, with some syrupiness.

Palate Less subtlety but more Highland character.

Finish More emphatic.

SCORE 76

DEANSTON

Distillery rating ☆☆   **Producer** Burn Stewart
Region Highlands   **District** Midlands

I N THE HIGHLANDS but only by a few miles. South-west of Perth, beyond Crieff and Gleneagles, is Doune, with a well-preserved medieval castle and an historic former cotton mill designed by Richard Arkwright. The mill was originally water driven, and is on the river Teith. The supply of good water apparently contributed to the decision to turn the mill into a distillery, at a time when the whisky industry was doing very well. It opened as the Deanston distillery in 1965/6, with the vaulted weaving shed as a warehouse. The distillery prospered during the 1970s, but closed during the difficult mid 1980s. At the time, it was owned by Invergordon. With the revival of the industry in the late '80s and early '90s, Deanston was bought by the blenders Burn Stewart. It is hoped that, as a result, this pleasant malt will become more readily available. A 1977 sample (at 55 vol) from the Scotch Malt Whisky Society was promisingly rich in its toffeeish maltiness.

DEANSTON, no age statement, 40 vol
Colour Pale.
Nose Fresh, lightly sweet aroma, with some dryness at the back of the nose.
Body Light, smooth.
Palate Well balanced; notes of sweet maltiness and fruitiness.
Finish Light, medium-dry finish.

SCORE 69

DUFFTOWN

Distillery rating ☆☆☆ **Producer** United Distillers
Region Highlands **District** Speyside (Dufftown)

THE EARL OF FIFE, James Duff, laid out the eponymous town, where the rivers Fiddich and Dullan meet on their way to the Spey. It is pronounced "Dufton", and has seven malt distilleries. Only one appropriates Dufftown as its name, and in past manifestations confusingly tagged on the word Glenlivet. In fact, Dufftown is some distance from the glen of the Livet, and has no need anyway for such devices. Speyside distilleries used to believe that a murmured reference to Glenlivet added a cachet, but these allusions are gradually vanishing. The Dufftown distillery and its next-door-neighbour Pittyvaich were both owned by Bells until that company was acquired by what is now United Distillers. Dufftown's stone-built premises were originally a meal mill, in 1896, but they have since sprouted a pagoda, and were twice expanded in the 1970s. Dufftown's malt is a good, no-nonsense Highland whisky.

DUFFTOWN Eight-year-old, 40 vol

Colour Full, golden.

Nose Lightly aromatic, with hints of smoke and plenty of malty dryness.

Body Medium; rounded, firm and dryish.

Palate Seems to promise more than it delivers.
Again, suggestions of smoke and a lot of malty dryness.

Finish A lingering viscosity on the tongue but not a great deal of flavour.

SCORE 70

DUFFTOWN 10-year-old, 40 vol

Colour Full, golden.

Nose A little more of everything. Very well rounded.

Body Much more viscosity.

Palate Quite syrupy.

Finish Lacks flavour development.

SCORE 71

DUFFTOWN 15-year-old, 43 vol (cask sample)

Colour Pale golden.

Nose Assertively aromatic.

Body Lightly syrupy.

Palate Malty, on the dry side, becoming flowery.

Finish Lingers, but very light.

SCORE 71

EDRADOUR

Distillery rating ☆☆☆☆　　**Producer** Campbell Distillers
Region Highlands　　**District** Midlands

T HE SMALLEST DISTILLERY in Scotland. Edradour is the last original "farm" distillery, with some very traditional equipment. It likes to trace its history back to the beginning of legal whisky production in the Highlands, in 1825, though the present distillery is believed to have been founded in 1837. The distillery is at the hamlet of Balnauld, above the town of Pitlochry. This small, remote distillery is reputed to have done a busy trade with American customers during Prohibition. A story that it was later indirectly owned for a lengthy period by the Mafia has not been substantiated. It produces as much malt whisky in a year as some distilleries can make in a week, and has a staff of three. Its water rises through peat and granite, reaching the surface a few hundred yards from the distillery. The company says it uses local barley. Its stills are the smallest in Scotland, and that must contribute to the distinctive richness of the malt. Stills any smaller than those at Edradour would not be permitted by Customs and Excise, for fear that they could be operated in a secret hiding place. In the late 1980s, Edradour began to bottle its whisky as a 10-year-old single malt under its own label. Before then, the Edradour whisky had been the defining component of a fuller, vatted malt called Glenforres.

This classically pretty distillery is hidden in a glen. The approaching visitor crests a hill, and suddenly there it is in the hollow below.

EDRADOUR 10-year-old, 40 vol

Colour Full golden.

Nose Peppermint, sugared almonds, hint of sherry, spicy-smoky notes.

Body Remarkably creamy texture for a relatively light malt.

Palate Minty-clean, creamy, malty.

Finish Mellow, warming.

SCORE 81

EDRADOUR 1973, 40 vol, Gordon and MacPhail

Colour Bronze.

Nose More sherry character.

Body Light, but smooth and rounded.

Palate More nutty maltiness. Astonishingly creamy.

Finish Warming, enveloping, long.

SCORE 85

EDRADOUR 1968, 46 vol, Signatory

Colour Golden.

Nose Perfumy, dry.

Body Light but firm, oily.

Palate Very nutty (walnuts?), flowery, dry.

Finish Dry and rather abrupt.

SCORE 80

FETTERCAIRN

Distillery rating ☆☆☆ **Producer** Whyte and Mackay
Region Highlands **District** Eastern Highlands

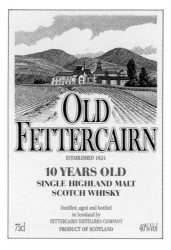

OLD
FETTERCAIRN
ESTABLISHED 1824
10 YEARS OLD
SINGLE HIGHLAND MALT
SCOTCH WHISKY
Distilled, aged and bottled
in Scotland by
FETTERCAIRN DISTILLERS COMPANY
PRODUCT OF SCOTLAND
75cl   40%Vol

BETWEEN THE CAIRNGORMS and the sea, the peaks, forests and glens hid a number of distilleries on the old whisky routes to the ports of the east coast. The village and distillery of Fettercairn are near the glen of the North Esk, a river that flows into the sea not far from the town of Montrose. Fettercairn is one of Scotland's oldest distilleries, reputed to have been founded in 1824. It was rebuilt several times around the turn of the century, and extended in 1966. The single malt is subtle, and easy to underrate. It has now been promoted from an eight-year-old to a 10. A dash of sherry, a couple more years, and perhaps the marginally higher alcohol, make a difference. The earthiness of the nutty character is less obvious, but there is more character all round.

OLD FETTERCAIRN 10-year-old, 40 vol

Colour Very full gold.

Nose A hint of sherry. Nutty. Faint peat? Very appetizing.

Body Light, smooth, silky.

Palate Nutty dryness and a toffeeish (but elusive, light, clean) sweetness, beautifully balanced.

Finish Gentle, with a clean sweetness, becoming perfumy. Lingering, very warm.

SCORE 77

GLEN ALBYN

Distillery rating ☆☆ **Producer** United Distillers
Region Highlands **District** Speyside (Inverness)

CONNOISSEURS CHOICE

Connoisseurs Choice, a range of single malts from various districts of Scotland.

In the Highlands are situated the greatest number of malt whisky distilleries.

SINGLE HIGHLAND
MALT SCOTCH WHISKY
DISTILLED AT
GLEN ALBYN
DISTILLERY
PROPRIETORS: Mackinlay & Birnie Ltd

DISTILLED **1968** DISTILLED

SPECIALLY SELECTED, PRODUCED AND BOTTLED BY
75cl GORDON & MACPHAIL 40%vol
ELGIN · SCOTLAND
PRODUCT OF SCOTLAND

T HE CITY OF INVERNESS is regarded as the capital of the Highlands, and is a good base from which to tour Speyside. A distillery in Inverness itself would be on the edge of Speyside, but would perhaps qualify for the appellation. The city had three distilleries, all of which have been closed for some years, though their malts can be found in independent bottlings. Glen Albyn was founded in 1846, closed in the early 1980s and has since been demolished.

GLEN ALBYN 1968, 40 vol, Gordon and MacPhail (cask sample)

Colour Amber.

Nose Faintly spirity, flowery. Hint of sherry.

Body Medium, firm.

Palate Sherryish, oaky, nutty, malty. Flavours tightly combined.

Finish Very long indeed, with a warm wisp of smokiness.

SCORE 71

Other versions of Glen Albyn

A Signatory 1964 (58 vol) was spirity in the nose, but more perfumy and flowery in the palate. SCORE 70.

GLENALLACHIE

Distillery rating ☆☆☆　**Producer** Campbell Distillers
Region Highlands　**District** Speyside

GLENALLACHIE IS IN THE HEART of Speyside, near Aberlour. A dam that looks like a village pond, and a small waterfall, soften the exterior of what is otherwise a functional modern distillery. It was built in 1967, primarily to contribute malt to the Mackinlay blends, at that time owned by Scottish and Newcastle Breweries. In 1985, the distillery and the Mackinlay business was acquired by Invergordon. The distillery was temporarily closed in the late 1980s, but acquired and reopened by Campbell at the end of the decade. The malt has never been well known, but deserves a greater reputation. Glenallachie is a superb example of a subtle, complex, Speyside whisky of the delicate type. It is pronounced "Glen-alec-y".

GLENALLACHIE 12-year-old, 43 vol
An elegant, graceful, pre-dinner companion.

Colour Very pale.

Nose Fragrant, lightly sweet and malty.

Body Light but firm.

Palate Beautifully clean, smooth and delicate.

Finish Starts sweet and develops toward a long perfumy finish.

SCORE 76

GLENBURGIE

Distillery rating ☆☆ **Producer** Allied Distillers
Region Highlands **District** Speyside (Findhorn)

AT THE WATERSHED of the Findhorn, between Forres and Elgin, this distillery produces distinctively herbal-tasting malts that contribute to the Ballantine blends, but are hard to find as single malts. There have been occasional "official" bottlings of the Glenburgie malt at five-years-old, but it is not regularly available in this form. Independent bottlings of Glenburgie can also sometimes be found at other ages. Despite its somewhat distant location, the distillery uses the appelation Gelnburgie-Glenlivet. A distillery was founded on the site, at Alves, in 1829, subsequently fell into disuse, was revived in 1878, and extended in 1958. At that time, two Lomond stills were added. The whisky made in the Lomond stills has never been released as a single malt in "official" bottlings. Independent bottlings were made, under the name Glencraig, and can still be found, though stocks are finite: the Lomond stills were removed in the early 1980s.

GLENBURGIE 1968, 40 vol, Gordon and MacPhail

Colour Gold.
Nose Dry, herbal, fruity.
Body Light, smooth, becoming syrupy.
Palate Sweet, with some bourbon character, vanilla and perhaps even cinnamon.
Finish Long, warming.

SCORE 68

CONNOISSEURS
CHOICE

Connoisseurs Choice, a
range of single malts from
various districts of
Scotland.

The distilleries situated in
the area of the valley of the
River Spey produce some of
the finest malt whiskies.

SINGLE SPEYSIDE
MALT SCOTCH WHISKY
DISTILLED AT
GLENCRAIG
DISTILLERY
PROPRIETORS: Jas. & Geo. Stodart Ltd
DISTILLED 1970 DISTILLED
SPECIALLY SELECTED, PRODUCED AND BOTTLED BY
75cl   GORDON & MACPHAIL   40%vol
ELGIN · SCOTLAND
PRODUCT OF SCOTLAND

GLENCRAIG 1970, 40 vol, Gordon and MacPhail

Colour Bright gold.

Nose Dry but powerfully fruity (tropical fruit? Guava, perhaps?), especially after a dash of water has been added.

Body Firm, oily.

Finish Some syrupy sweetness, then a pear-brandy dryness. Very long, dry, slightly woody. A rare and exotic after-dinner malt.

SCORE 68

GLENCADAM

Distillery rating ☆☆   **Producer** Allied Distillers
Region Highlands   **District** Eastern Highlands

CONNOISSEURS CHOICE

Connoisseurs Choice, a range of single malts from various districts of Scotland.

In the Highlands are situated the greatest number of malt whisky distilleries.

SINGLE HIGHLAND MALT SCOTCH WHISKY
DISTILLED AT
GLENCADAM
DISTILLERY
PROPRIETORS: Geo. Ballantine & Son Ltd

DISTILLED **1974** DISTILLED

SPECIALLY SELECTED, PRODUCED AND BOTTLED BY
75cl   **GORDON & MACPHAIL**   40% vol
ELGIN · SCOTLAND
PRODUCT OF SCOTLAND

THIS WELL-TENDED DISTILLERY is in a pretty location just outside the ancient city and market town of Brechin, on the east coast. The distillery was founded in 1825 and extensively modernised in 1959. It has been associated with Ballantine and Stewart's Cream of the Barley blend. The latter seems appropriate, as Glencadam is an unusually creamy malt. It is bottled by Gordon and MacPhail. There is also a limited edition bottling from Stewart's in a crystal decanter.

GLENCADAM 1974, 40 vol, Gordon and MacPhail

Colour Full.
Nose Smoky-fruity.
Body Full, creamy.
Palate Fresh, with some malty, buttery sweetness.
Finish Warming.

SCORE 68

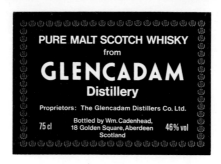

PURE MALT SCOTCH WHISKY
from
GLENCADAM
Distillery
Proprietors: The Glencadam Distillers Co. Ltd.
75 cl   Bottled by Wm. Cadenhead,
18 Golden Square, Aberdeen
Scotland   46% vol

GLENCADAM, 21-year-old, 46 vol, Cadenhead (cask sample)

Colour Full gold.

Nose Powerful, aromatic, smoky-fruity.

Body Full, drying on the tongue.

Palate Sweet. Strawberries and ice-cream.

Finish Warming, notes of bourbon.

SCORE 68

GLEN DEVERON

Distillery rating ☆☆☆   **Producer** William Lawson Distillers
Region Highlands   **District** Speyside (Deveron)

A NEOPHYTE WISHING TO LEARN the true aroma and taste of malt (the raw material, as well as its distillate) could do worse than work for a few evenings on a bottle of Glen Deveron. This is a clean, uncluttered, malty whisky that is very easy to drink and enjoy. It is also a single malt that is becoming more readily available – as Glen Deveron 12-year-old. The Deveron is the river valley and district on the eastern edge of Speyside. The distillery, on the banks of the river, is called Macduff, and looks across the river to the town of Banff. The whisky appears under the name Macduff in some independent bottlings. The distillery was built in 1962, and is operated by William Lawson Distillers, who have links through General Beverage with the international Martini and Rossi group. The malt no doubt finds it way into the William Lawson's blend.

GLEN DEVERON 12-year-old, 40 vol

Colour Gold.

Nose Hints of sherry and sweet maltiness in a fresh, appetizing aroma.

Body Light to medium, but notably smooth.

Palate Full, very clean, maltiness.

Finish Malty dryness; quick, but pleasantly warming.

SCORE 75

MACDUFF 1975, 40 vol, Gordon and MacPhail

Colour Amber.

Nose Hints of sherry (fino?).

Body Light to medium.

Palate Slightly sulphury.

Finish Quick.

SCORE 70

MACDUFF 21-year-old, 55.5 vol, James MacArthur

Colour Yellowy gold.

Nose More sherry than colour suggests. Hint of sweet maltiness.

Body Light to medium, but very smooth and oily.

Palate Lots of flavour development. Soft and malty, moving to a sappy dryness; then a flowery sweetness.

Finish A little longer.

SCORE 76

GLENDRONACH

Distillery rating ☆☆☆   **Producer** Allied Distillers
Region Highlands   **District** Speyside (Deveron)

A UNIQUE CHOICE of versions aged in different woods. One, with a maroon-tinted label, is identified as having been matured in sherry casks. The other version, with a green-tinged label, is described as "original". This is aged in a mixture of sherry and plain wood. "Plain" wood may be sherry casks that have been used several times for whisky, or Bourbon barrels. In either version, Glendronach is a sweet, rich, malty whisky. The choice offers the devotee the chance to test the impact of sherry ageing. The distillery's parent company, Teacher's, has in recent years made several innovative moves in labelling. Its regular blended whisky announces on the label that at least 45 percent of its content is malt. Teacher's also has a super-premium blend, called Reserve Stock, that is guaranteed to contain at least 60 percent malt. Both of these percentages are higher than is customarily found in competing products. William Teacher was a wine and spirit merchant during the 19th century, and he was noted for his blended whiskies. The Glendronach distillery was founded in 1826 but was not acquired by Teacher's until 1960. Teacher's later became part of Allied. Glendronach has a floor maltings, and coal-fired stills. The distillery is east of Huntly and south of the river Deveron, on the very edge of Speyside.

The Glendronach distillery is set in rich Aberdeenshire farming country.

GLENDRONACH original, 12-year-old, 43 vol

Colour Gold.

Nose Dry, with a hint of sherry, and lots of maltiness.

Body Medium to full. Very smooth and slightly syrupy.

Palate The malt is well balanced by heathery dryness.

Finish Big development of flavour, with clean, fruity, perfumy notes characteristic of this malt.

SCORE 75

GLENDRONACH matured in sherry casks, 12-year-old, 40 vol

Colour Very deep amber.

Nose Intense sherry (sweet oloroso?).

Body Very rich and luscious.

Palate A good balance of sherry character and maltiness. Some caramel-like sweetness, though by no means overpowering.

Finish Very long, with some dryness.

SCORE 77

GLENDRONACH 18-year-old, 43 vol
(There has also been a limited edition at 19 years old.)

Colour A bright, extremely deep, amber.

Nose Plenty of sherry, but also a burnt-toffee dryness and a hint of smoke.

Body Smooth, slightly drying.

Palate Starts with burnt-toffee dryness, moves to malty sweetness, then to sherry.

Finish Long, smooth, warming, with some toffeeish dryness.

SCORE 79

GLENDULLAN

Distillery rating ☆☆☆   **Producer** United Distillers
Region Highlands   **District** Speyside (Dufftown)

AN UNDERRATED, and not especially well-known, malt that is worth sampling. It was supplied to King Edward VII in 1902, and for some years afterwards proclaimed this on its casks. Glendullan is one of several malts associated with the Old Parr blends, which originated from Macdonald Greenlees. A bottling over the Macdonald Greenlees name has a good dash of sherry. A newer bottling in the United Distillers "flora and fauna" series has more distillery character. The distillery was founded in 1897 and expanded in 1972.

GLENDULLAN 12-year-old, 43 vol
A big, assertive, after-dinner malt. Or put it in a hip-flask.

Colour Amber.
Nose Some sherry, malty, lightly perfumy and fruity.
Body Medium to full; smooth, firm and silky.
Palate Powerful, dry and malty, with perfumy, fruity notes developing.
Finish Firm, long, warming.

SCORE 75

GLENDULLAN 12-year-old, 43 vol (cask sample)
Starts modestly, but the finish is remarkable. A malt to savour.

Colour Almost white, with just a tinge of gold.

Nose Light, dry, maltiness. Hint of fruit.

Body Medium. Firm. Silky.

Palate Dry start, becoming malty, nutty, perfumy and lightly fruity.

Finish Extraordinarily perfumy and long.

SCORE 75

GLENDULLAN 22-year-old, 46 vol, Cadenhead (cask sample)

Colour Pale golden.

Nose Dry, assertive.

Body Medium to full, drying on the tongue.

Palate More sweetness and perfume. Less well-balanced.

Finish Perfumy, warming.

SCORE 74

GLEN ELGIN

Distillery rating ☆☆☆   **Producer** United Distillers
Region Highlands   **District** Speyside (Lossie)

WHITE HORSE
GLEN ELGIN
SINGLE HIGHLAND MALT
SCOTCH WHISKY

DISTILLED AND BOTTLED IN SCOTLAND BY
WHITE HORSE DISTILLERS, GLASGOW, SCOTLAND

750 ml   GLEN ELGIN DISTILLERY, ELGIN, MORAYSHIRE   43% vol

WHERE THE RIVER LOSSIE approaches the malt whisky town of Elgin, there are no fewer than eight distilleries within a few miles. Glen Elgin is not the nearest to the town whose name it bears, but close enough. There are some excellent whiskies in this stretch of country and the sweetish Glen Elgin is one of them. The distillery was founded in 1898–1900, rebuilt and extended in 1964. The malt is an important component of the White Horse blended whisky. Glen Elgin has been available as a 12-year-old single malt in an official bottling for some years. In 1991, a new official bottling was introduced, still at 12 years old, but with no age statement on the label. The new bottling seems fractionally paler, slightly less smoky in the nose, with some dryish sherry notes.

GLEN ELGIN, no age statement, 43 vol
Colour Medium gold.
Nose Heather honey.
Body Light to medium.
Palate Dryish, flowery, start; becoming sweet, honeyish clean and malty; developing a dash of tangerine-like fruitiness.
Finish Smooth, becoming drier again, with late notes of smoke and sherry.

SCORE 76

GLENESK

Distillery rating ☆☆☆   **Producer** United Distillers
Region Highlands **District** Eastern Highlands

ALTHOUGH IT IS BOTTLED under the distillery label, this fresh, clean, lightly malty whisky can be hard to find as a single malt. Traditionally, it has been an important component of the blended whisky VAT 69, bottled in South Queensferry, near Edinburgh, by William Sanderson, formerly a Distillers Company Limited subsidiary and now subsumed into United Distillers. The Glenesk distillery is at the mouth of the South Esk river, at Montrose. It began its life as a flax mill and became a malt distillery in 1897. It was re-equipped to produce grain whisky around the time of the Second World War, converted back in the 1960s, and extended in the 1970s. It has been temporarily closed since 1985. Despite its chequered history, it has very much the look of a traditional malt distillery. It has an adjoining maltings, of the drum type.

GLENESK 12-year-old, 40 vol
Colour Gold.
Nose Dry maltiness, aromatic, with some restrained, balancing, sweetness.
Body Light to medium, soft, smooth.
Palate Soft and pleasant. Dry maltiness, with some balancing notes of restrained sweetness.
Finish An aromatic, dry maltiness throughout makes for an unusual, clean, fresh, malt.

SCORE 66

GLENFARCLAS

Distillery rating ☆☆☆☆   **Producer** J. and G. Grant
Region Highlands   **District** Speyside

OUTSTANDING MALTS, and in an unusually wide variety of ages. Experienced tasters usually place them in the top three or four from this most distinguished district. The Glenfarclas malts are at the heftier end of the Speyside line-up, though they are not the very heaviest. They are also emphatically in the well-sherried style. In both respects, they are less assertive than The Macallan, with which they are often compared. The Glenfarclas malts are the strong, silent type: tall, dark and handsome, notably firm-bodied, but willing to reveal a sweet side to their nature. They are excellent company at any time, and especially after dinner. Glenfarclas means "valley of the green grass". The distillery is about a mile from the Spey, and set on a cattle farm, just beyond which the heather-covered hills rise toward Ben Rinnes from which the distillery's water flows. There is also barley grown in the surrounding area. The distillery grew out of the farm. The site, variously known simply as Glenfarclas, or as Rechlerich, is not far from the village of Marypark, in the Ballindalloch area.

The distillery is large and successful, but it is not part of a group. It is the business of a wholly private, family-owned company, J. and G. Grant. They are not connected (except perhaps distantly) to any of the other whisky-making Grants, and regard theirs as the most truly independent of all Scottish

distilleries. The distillery was founded in 1836, and has been in the family since 1865. Its still-house is modern, and its stills the biggest on Speyside. They are heated by gas flame. A substantial proportion of the whisky is aged in first-use sherry casks, some in re-fill sherry casks, and some in plain wood.

The Glenfarclas distillery signs itself with a flourish, together with a reminder of its great age.

GLENFARCLAS, no age statement, 60 vol

Known as 105°, from the old British proof system. This is the strongest single malt offered by any distillery in an "official" bottling. Although it no longer carries an age statement, it is eight to 10 years old. A very youthful version for such a big malt, but with all the muscle of the high proof, which is virtually cask strength.

Colour Bronze.

Nose Big and uncomplicated; raisins, butterscotch, toffee.

Body Full, heavy.

Palate Very sweet, rich ... nectar.

Finish Long, and warmed by that high proof. This is one to accompany a slice of fruit cake. Extra points for cheeky, youthful individuality.

SCORE 88

GLENFARCLAS 10-year-old, 40 vol

Elegant, and quite dry for a Glenfarclas.

Colour Bronze.

Nose Big, with some sherry sweetness, but also smokiness at the back of the nose.

Body Characteristically firm.

Palate Crisp and dry at first, with the flavour filling out as it develops.

Finish Sweet and long.

SCORE 86

GLENFARCLAS 12-year-old, 43 vol
For many devotees, the most familiar face of Glenfarclas.

Colour Bronze.	
Nose Drier, with a quick, big attack.	
Body Firm, slightly oily.	
Palate Plenty of flavour, with notes of peat-smoke.	
Finish Long, with oaky notes, even at this relatively young age.	

SCORE 87

GLENFARCLAS 15-year-old, 46 vol
Many enthusiasts feel that the 15-year-old most deftly demonstrates the complexity of this malt. Certainly the best-balanced Glenfarclas.

Colour Amber.

Nose Plenty of sherry, oak, maltiness, and a hint of smokiness … all the elements in a lovely, mixed bouquet.

Body Firm, rounded..

Palate Assertive, with all the elements again beautifully melded.

Finish Long and smooth.

SCORE 88

GLENFARCLAS 18-year-old, 46 vol, Cadenhead (cask sample)

Colour Pale amber.

Nose Powerful, long, some smokiness.

Body Big, firm. Fills the mouth.

Palate Oaky and sweet.

Finish Sweet, some sherry, a dash of oak, very powerful and long.

SCORE 88

GLENFARCLAS 21-year-old, 43 vol

Colour Amber.

Nose More sherry and a greater smokiness, as well as a dash of oak, all slowly emerging as distinct notes.

Body Big, firm.

Palate Immense flavour development, bringing out many more notes.

Finish Remarkably long, with lots of sherry.
Becoming sweetish and perfumy.

SCORE 89

GLENFARCLAS 25-year-old, 43 vol
More of everything. Perhaps a touch woody for purists,
but a remorselessly serious after-dinner malt for others.

Colour Dark amber.

Nose Pungent, sappy.

Body Big, with some dryness of texture.

Palate The flavours are so tightly interlocked at first that the whisky appears reluctant to give up its secrets. Very slow, insistent flavour development. All the components gradually emerge, but in a drier mood.

Finish Long, oaky, sappy. Extra points out of respect for idiosyncratic age.

SCORE 88

Other versions of Glenfarclas
As compared to the official 15-year-old, an Avery's 1967 (bottled '83) had much less sherry, and interestingly revealed a flowery-nutty distillery character. SCORE 86. A Signatory 1969 vintage, at 58.2 vol, is splendidly sherryish. SCORE 89. There have also been some very good bottlings from the Scotch Malt Whisky Society.

GLENFIDDICH

Distillery rating ☆☆☆   **Producer** William Grant and Sons
Region Highlands   **District** Speyside (Dufftown)

THE GLEN OF THE RIVER FIDDICH gives its name to the biggest-selling single malt whisky in the world. The Glenfiddich distillery is on the small river whose name it bears, in Dufftown. Nearby, the Fiddich and river Dullan meet before joining the Spey. The name Fiddich indicates that the river runs in the valley of the deer. A stag is the company's emblem.

Glenfiddich spent some time waiting to be discovered. The distillery was founded in 1886/7, and is still in the original family, as a limited company. Nonetheless, it made an early start in the business of bottled single malts.

As a small, family company, it began to face intense competition from bigger names during the economic boom after the Second World War. In 1963, it decided to market its whisky seriously as a single malt, and to do so outside Scotland. For many years afterwards, companies in the industry continued to regard this as foolishness. The received wisdom of the whisky business was that single malts were too intense in palate for the English and other foreigners.

The vision and persistence of the company was in more than one sense single-minded. It was an example and precedent, without which few of its rivals would have been emboldened to offer themselves as bottled single malts. Devotees of the genre owe a debt of gratitude to Glenfiddich.

The early start laid the foundations for the success of Glenfiddich. The fact that it is, among malts, one of the less challenging to the palate, undoubtedly also helped a great deal. Glenfiddich in its usual form (no age statement, but customarily eight-years-old) is very easily drinkable: a light, smooth malt, with a hint of fruitiness. It is labelled Special Old Reserve. Devotees of malts who are ready for a greater challenge will find more complexity, at a price, in the elaborately packaged 18-, 21- and 30-year-old versions that are now available. The company also owns the long-established Balvenie and new Kininvie malt distilleries. The principal malt may be close to the mainstream, but the distillery is full of character. Much of the original structure, in honey-and-grey stone, remains, beautifully maintained, and the style has been followed in considerable new construction. Although the distillery no longer produces its own malt, pagodas have been added to some of the newer buildings as a salute – however coy – to tradition.

A truly traditional element is the use of coal-fired stills. The stills are small, and the whisky is principally aged in plain oak, though about 10 percent goes into sherry casks. Whisky aged in different woods is married in plain oak. Glenfiddich likes jokingly to describe its malt as "Château-bottled". The distillery is unusual in that it has its own bottling line on the premises. The only other malt distillery with bottling facilities is Springbank, where a very small line is also used for the Cadenhead range.

William Grant no longer sells whisky for blending under the Glenfiddich name, the intention being to ensure that the company can guarantee the origin of any whisky bearing this name. Like several other distillers, the company also feels that its label should be used only on whisky aged according to its own practices. Cadenhead, however, has marketed some older ages of single malt whisky under the name Glenfiddich-Glenlivet.

The handsome steeply pitched roofs and traditional pagoda shape of distillery maltings at the Glenfiddich distillery.

GLENFIDDICH Special Old Reserve, no age statement, 40 vol

Colour Very pale, "white wine".

Nose Light, fresh but sweet, appetizing, fruity, pear-like.

Body Light, lean, firm, smooth.

Palate Dryish. Pear-like. More fruitiness as flavour develops. A dash of water releases a hint of smokiness and some sweet, malty notes.

Finish Restrained, aromatic.

SCORE 75

Spode presentation decanter with hand-stamped seal

GLENFIDDICH 18-year-old, 43 vol

Colour Full gold.

Nose Softer, richer.

Body Much softer.

Palate Much more mellow and rounded, soft, restrained.

Finish Dryish. A hint of peat?

SCORE 78

Wedgwood Jasper-ware presentation decanter.

GLENFIDDICH 21-year-old, 43 vol

Colour Full gold, fractionally darker.

Nose Hint of sherry?

Body Surprisingly full.

Palate Complex, with both sweetness and dryness. Eventually, the dry notes are more assertive, with a hint of peat.

Finish Still gentle but longer.

SCORE 81

Limited edition Edinburgh crystal decanter with silver stag head stopper.

GLENFIDDICH 30-year-old, 43 vol

Colour Full gold, fractionally darker still.

Nose Notes of sherry, fruit, chocolate and ginger.

Body Soft, full, some viscosity.

Palate More sherry, raisins, chocolate, ginger. Luxurious.

Finish Unhurried, with chocolatey notes and gingery dryness.

SCORE 86

Other versions of Glenfiddich

Cadenhead bottlings at 22- and 24-years-old may be found in the odd bar, restaurant or shop. The 22-year-old is dry, malty and aromatic, with a full body and sweet, gingerish palate. The 24-year-old is very sweet, with hints of sherry.

GLEN GARIOCH

Distillery rating ☆☆☆☆   **Producer** Morrison Bowmore
Region Highlands   **District** Eastern Highlands

BETWEEN SPEYSIDE and the east coast, Glen Garioch (pronounced "Geery") is the Highland partner of the Lowland malt Auchentoshan and the island malt Bowmore. These three distilleries share an owner, and each makes excellent malts. Glen Garioch is the assertive peat-smoky style of Highland malt that has become all too rare. The distillery is on the road from Banff to Aberdeen, at the quaintly named town of Old Meldrum, in the sheltered Garioch valley, traditionally the grain-growing district for this part of Scotland. The distillery, founded in 1798, is a chunky, stone building that looks in parts like a village school. It is very traditional in that it has floor maltings, but innovative in the manner in which it has sought to re-use the heat generated in the distilling process. The heat is used to warm greenhouses in which a variety of flowers and salad items have been grown and ripened.

GLEN GARIOCH Eight-year-old, 43 vol

Colour Full, gold.

Nose Faintly smoky, heathery, flowery.

Body Medium, firm.

Palate Light smokiness, dryness, slightly spirity notes. Developing to a light, malty, raisiny, sweetness.

Finish Quick and warming.

> SCORE 76

GLEN GARIOCH 10-year-old, 43 vol
A good introduction to peat smoke.

Colour Full, gold.

Nose Lightly smoky, with a good depth of aroma.

Body Medium, firm.

Palate Smokiness, then some raisiny sweetness, developing into a tasty, malty character.

Finish Quick, smoky-dry and warming.

SCORE 77

GLEN GARIOCH 21-year-old, 43 vol (cask sample)
A robust malt that deserves to be better known.

Colour Pale gold.

Nose Definitely smoky.

Body Medium to full.

Palate Much more intense, very sweet in the middle, and well rounded.

Finish Big and very smoky, but smooth. Lots of lingering fragrance.

SCORE 80

Other versions of Glen Garioch
Cask-strength, sherry-aged versions sampled at the Scotch Malt Whisky Society have rated "majestic" from tasters there.

GLENGLASSAUGH

Distillery rating ☆☆☆ **Producer** Highland Distilleries
Region Highlands **District** Speyside (Deveron)

"**S**ACKCLOTH ... HESSIAN" proclaimed one taster, admiring the distinctive aroma of this malt. Flax, perhaps? Fresh linen? Newly-made beds? "Gorse ... broom" says another admirer. It is certainly an individualistic whisky, and inspires flights of fancy, if not Tom Jonesian fantasy – maybe it is the aroma of seaside sand dunes, covered with rough grass and gorse. This is a seaside malt, produced near Portsoy, on the coast of Speyside. The distillery is between the Spey and the river Deveron, just a little closer to the latter. It was founded in 1875, bought by Highland Distilleries in the 1890s, and completely rebuilt in 1960. It has been temporarily closed since the mid 1980s. The single malt is not widely available. In some countries it carries a 12-year age statement. The whisky has also contributed to blends like The Famous Grouse, Cutty Sark and Laing's.

Estd 1875
FINE HIGHLAND MALT

Glenglassaugh Distillery c.1875

GLENGLASSAUGH
SINGLE MALT SCOTCH WHISKY
BOTTLED IN SCOTLAND

75cl   DISTILLED AT   40%vol.
GLENGLASSAUGH DISTILLERY, PORTSOY, SCOTLAND

GLENGLASSAUGH no age statement, 40 vol

Colour Gold.

Nose Fresh linen.

Body Light but firm and smooth.

Palate Grassy, sweetish.

Finish Gentle, drying slightly.

SCORE 76

CONNOISSEURS CHOICE

Connoisseurs Choice, a range of single malts from various districts of Scotland.

In the Highlands are situated the greatest number of malt whisky distilleries.

SINGLE HIGHLAND
MALT SCOTCH WHISKY
DISTILLED AT
GLENGLASSAUGH
DISTILLERY
PROPRIETORS: The Highland Distilleries Ltd
DISTILLED 1967 DISTILLED
SPECIALLY SELECTED, PRODUCED AND BOTTLED BY
75cl GORDON & MACPHAIL 40%vol
ELGIN · SCOTLAND
PRODUCT OF SCOTLAND

GLENGLASSAUGH 1967, 40 vol, Gordon and MacPhail

Colour Full gold.

Nose Fresh, grassy.

Body Light to medium.

Palate Complex, drier, but with notes of sweet grassiness, heather-honey, peaches.

Finish Gentle, dry, warming, long-lasting.

SCORE 77

GLENGOYNE

Distillery rating ☆☆☆   **Producer** Lang Brothers
Region Highlands   **District** Western Highlands

AN EMINENTLY VISITABLE DISTILLERY, just over a dozen miles from the centre of Glasgow, and six or seven from Loch Lomond. Its home hamlet, Dumgoyne, is just across the Highland line. The distillery is in the valley of a small river that eventually flows into the loch. Sheep graze on the hills behind, and burns flow into a well-tended glen, forming a waterfall into the red sandstone hollow where ducks swim in the distillery's dam. It is said to have been established in 1833, and was earlier known as Burn Foot or Glen Guin. It has been owned by Lang's since the 1870s. Since the mid 1960s (when the distillery was extended) Lang's has been a subsidiary of Robertson and Baxter. That company in turn has links with Highland Distillers, whose subsidiary Matthew Gloag produces The Famous Grouse. As a single malt, Glengoyne has begun to be marketed more purposefully in recent years, and is quietly winning admirers. For a relatively light malt, and even at the younger ages, it has a lot of depth, and it is notable for its roundness and fruitiness. About a third of the malt is aged in sherry casks.

GLENGOYNE 10-year-old, 40 vol

Colour Full gold.

Nose A fresh but very soft, warm, fruitiness, with hints of malty dryness and sherry.

Body Light to medium, smooth, rounded.

Palate Clean, sweetish, tasty, very pleasant.

Finish Still sweet, but drying slightly. Clean, appetizing.

SCORE 74

GLENGOYNE 12-year-old, 43 vol
Very similar indeed to the 10-year-old. A dash more of everything.

SCORE 75

GLENGOYNE 17-year-old, 43 vol

Colour Slightly fuller.

Nose More sherry and dryness.

Body Very firm. Markedly bigger in texture.

Palate Lots of depth of flavour, without its being rich or heavy.

Finish Long and sherryish.

SCORE 76

GLEN GRANT

Distillery rating ☆☆☆☆   **Producer** Seagram
Region Highlands   **District** Speyside (Rothes)

ONE OF THE GREAT MALTS, by common consent. Glen Grant has been sold as a bottled single malt since the first decade of this century. It was well known in Scotland long before pioneers like Glenfiddich began to open up the English and international markets. Glen Grant is among the world's biggest-selling single malts, but much of its sale is in the younger ages, in the important Italian market. With its typically herbal, hazelnut palate, Glen Grant combines easy drinkability with a dash of distinction. This is especially true of the 10-year-old version. The version with no age statement, which is the principal Glen Grant in Britain, generally contains malt of not less than eight- or nine-years-old. These two, and the 15-year-old, have undoubtedly introduced many instant converts to the pursuit of single malts. There are older versions from independent bottlers, including sherryish vintages under the Prime Malt label in America. Glen Grant was founded in 1840, and some of the original buildings remain. The distillery is set around a small courtyard, with turreted and gabled offices in the "Scottish baronial" style, probably dating from the 1880s. It is a quirky place, traditional in style despite expansions in the 1970s. Some of the stills are coal-fired.

The Glen Grant distillery is tucked away at the end of the main street of Rothes, one of the whisky towns of the Spey Valley.

GLEN GRANT Five-year-old, 40 vol

Colour Very pale, "white wine".

Nose Light, dry fruitiness, spirity.

Body Light, slightly sticky, almost resiny.

Palate Spirity. Pear-brandy.

Finish Fruity, quick.

SCORE 65

GLEN GRANT no age statement, 40 vol

Colour Gold.

Nose Fruity, flowery, nutty, faintly spirity.

Body Light but firm.

Palate Dry, slightly astringent at first, becoming soft and nutty.

Finish Herbal.

SCORE 74

GLEN GRANT 10-year-old, 43 vol
Glen Grant character without an obvious intervention of sherry.

Colour Full gold.

Nose Still dry, but much softer, with some sweetness.

Body Light to medium.

Palate Lightly sweet start, quickly becoming nutty and very dry.

Finish Very dry, with herbal notes.

SCORE 76

GLEN GRANT 15-year-old, 40 vol

Colour Medium amber.

Nose Some sherry.

Body Light to medium.

Palate Sherryish, soft and nutty, dry.

Finish Mellow, warming.

SCORE 80

GLEN GRANT 16-year-old, 46 vol, Cadenhead (cask sample)

Colour Fino sherry.	
Nose Appetizingly fruity. Dessert apples? Hazelnut?	
Body Light to medium, soft.	
Palate Hazelnuts. Grassy. Bamboo shoots?	
Finish Grassy, flowery.	

SCORE 77

GLEN GRANT 21-year-old, 40 vol, Gordon and MacPhail
Take it slowly, and appreciate the subtlety and development.

Colour Full amber-red.

Nose Lots of sherry.

Body Medium, soft.

Palate Sherryish sweetness at first, then malt and grassy-peaty notes, finally the nutty Glen Grant dryness.

Finish Lingering, flowery.

SCORE 81

GLEN GRANT 23-year-old, 46 vol, Cadenhead (cask sample)

Colour As red as a ripe apple.

Nose Powerful sherry. Appetizing.

Body Medium, soft.

Palate Lots of sherry, but the nutty dryness of the whisky still fights through.

Finish Overwhelmingly dry. Woody. Astringent.

SCORE 69

GLEN GRANT 25-year-old, 40 vol, Gordon and MacPhail
Not so much chess as wrist-wrestling, with the sherry coming out on top. A robust version.

Colour Dark.

Nose Lots of sherry.

Body Medium, firm.

Palate Dry oloroso character at first, then nutty dryness. A lot of depth.

Finish Deep, flowery, peaty.

SCORE 81

GLEN GRANT 26-year-old, 46 vol, Cadenhead

Colour Ripe plum? Almost opaque.

Nose Powerful sherry.

Body Medium, soft.

Palate Overwhelmed by the sherry.

Finish Astringent.

SCORE 66

GLEN GRANT 1964, 46 vol, Signatory

Colour Amber-red.

Nose Sherry, nutty dryness.

Body Medium, smooth.

Palate Sherryish, nutty, with some sappy woodiness.

Finish Gently dry, with some sherryish, woody notes.

SCORE 79

GLEN GRANT 1960, 40 vol
Less sherry, but a beautifully mellow, mature, malt.

Colour Medium amber.

Nose Some sherry.

Body Medium.

Palate Sherryish and sweet, with mellow nuttiness.

Finish Very long and sweet, with gradual development of
gentle dryness.

SCORE 81

GLEN KEITH

Distillery rating ☆☆　**Producer** Seagram (Chivas Brothers)
Region Highlands　**District** Speyside (Strathisla)

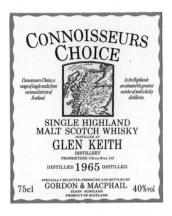

S EAGRAM HAS TWO DISTILLERIES next door to one another in the town of Keith, on the river Isla. One simply takes the name of the district, Strathisla. The other is Glen Keith, which was established on the site of a corn mill in 1957, during boom years for the industry. It was the first new malt distillery to have been founded in Scotland since a previous boom in late Victorian times. Glen Keith had the first gas-fired still in Scotland, and pioneered the use of computers in the industry. In its full name, the distillery adds the designation 'Glenlivet', like many of its contemporaries. As they own the original Glenlivet, not to mention Glen Grant – and Strathisla, for that matter – Seagrams have thus far not bottled Glen Keith as a single malt. In this form, its whisky is available only in independent bottlings. The malts of this district do tend to have a dryness that can seem woody, but the sample tasted may also have been rather long in the cask.

GLEN KEITH 1965, 40 vol, Gordon and MacPhail
Previous tastings of this malt have been sweeter and slightly chewier, though it has always had a dry finish. Clearly, it has dried with age.

Colour Bronze.
Nose Light, dry, hint of smoke. Slight woodiness.
Body Medium to full.
Palate Sweet, sherryish, start, quickly becoming drier; a hint of peat.
Finish Dry, long, warming.

SCORE 64

GLENKINCHIE

Distillery rating ☆☆☆☆ **Producer** United Distillers
Region Lowland **District** East

GLENKINCHIE IS NEAR the village of Pencaitland, only about 15 miles from Edinburgh, between the soft, green Lammermuir Hills and the small coastal resorts where the Firth of Forth meets the sea. It is in the glen of the Kinchie, a tributary of the Scottish river Tyne (not to be confused with the English one of the same name). The distillery – which has its own bowling green – is set in farmland. In the 1940s and 1950s, the distillery manager bred prize-winning cattle, feeding them on the spent grain. In 1968, the former floor maltings were turned into an early museum of malt whisky. Among the exhibits is a beautifully-crafted model of the distillery which was built in 1924 by the firm of Basset-Lowke, known for their model steam engines. It was constructed for the 1924 Empire Exhibition at Wembley, London. The distillery itself was founded in the 1830s and largely rebuilt between the two World Wars. Its whisky was launched as a bottled single in the Classic Malts range in 1988/9. It is a tasty, refreshing, malt after a walk in the hills.

GLENKINCHIE 10-year-old, 43 vol

Colour Gold.

Nose Soft, very sweetly aromatic, grassy sweetness, hint of smoke emerging after a time.

Body Light to medium, some viscosity.

Palate A very clean, grassy sweetness; smooth, well-defined, with lots of flavour development.

Finish Becoming spicy: cinnamon, ginger? Gentle, warming, dryish.

SCORE 76

GLENKINCHIE 21-year-old, 46 vol, Cadenhead (cask sample)

Colour Gold.

Nose Aromatic.

Body Light to medium, soft.

Palate Sweet, grassy.

Finish Grassy, aromatic.

SCORE 76

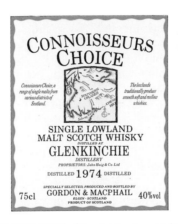

GLENKINCHIE 1974, 40 vol, Gordon and MacPhail
Probably bottled at more than 10-years-old, but the extra age does not seem to have made a lot of difference.

Colour Full gold.

Nose Suggestion of hickory smoke.

Body Light to medium, firm.

Palate Sweet, grassy, faintly smoky.

Finish Longer.

SCORE 76

THE GLENLIVET

Distillery rating ☆☆☆☆☆   **Producer** Seagram
Region Highlands   **District** Speyside (Livet)

WHAT GRANDE CHAMPAGNE is to Cognac, the glen of the river Livet is to Speyside. The only whisky allowed to call itself "The Glenlivet" is historically the most famous Speyside malt. The definite article is restricted even further, in that it appears on only the "official" bottlings from the owning company of The Glenlivet distillery, Seagram. These are branded as The Glenlivet, with the legend "Distilled by George & J.G. Smith" in small type at the bottom of the label, referring to the company set up by a father and son that originally founded the distillery.

The independent bottlers Gordon and MacPhail have made something of a speciality of older and vintage-dated examples, in a variety of alcoholic strengths, from the same distillery, and these are identified as George & J.G. Smith's Glenlivet Whisky. This range changes according to availability.

The glen of the Livet is also the home of two other malt distilleries: the unconnected Tamnavulin (see p. 214), and Braes of Glenlivet, which is owned by Seagram. In the adjoining Avon valley, the Tomintoul distillery (see p.221) is also generally regarded as belonging to the Livet district. It is, indeed, in the parish of Glenlivet. All of these distilleries use the sub-title Glenlivet on their labels as an appellation of district. So, stretching a point, do about a dozen from other parts of Speyside. This practice, which has declined somewhat, dates from the glen's pioneering position in commercial whisky production. Merchants in the cities wanted whisky "from Glenlivet" because that was the first specific producing district that they knew by name.

The malts that are produced in and immediately around the glen are all delicate and elegant. These characteristics are sometimes regarded as being the "glen" style. The malt from Braes of Glenlivet is not available as a bottled single. Among those that are bottled as singles, Tamnavulin is lightest in body, and Tomintoul in palate. Within this general style of delicate, elegant, malts, The Glenlivet has the most body and definition.

Opinion is divided as to how much its renown derives from history and how much from its character, but the latter should not be underrated. In blindfold tastings, it shows itself to be a complex malt. It is distilled from a water with a dash of hardness, and a mix of lightly and well-peated malts. About a third of the whisky is said to be matured in sherry wood.

Just as Grande Champagne rests on soil that grows the grapes best suited to Cognac, so the glen of the Livet has clean spring water that makes especially delicate whiskies. Among the distilling districts, it is the one most deeply set into the mountains. Its water rises from granite, and frequently flows underground for many miles. The mountain setting also provides for the weather that whisky-makers like. When distilling is in progress, the condensers work most effectively if they are cooled by very cold water, and in a climate to match.

The location also favoured illicit production in the days when commercial distilling was banned and is a significant reason for the renown of the glen. There are said to have been a couple of hundred illicit stills in the wild, mountain country around the Livet in the late 1700s and early 1800s. The district was also a haven for whisky-smugglers on their way over the mountains to the bigger cities and ports, in the Midlands and south of Scotland.

The modern face of the Glenlivet distillery conceals the older buildings, some of which date back to 1858, when the Smiths moved here.

At that time, partly because of grain shortages but also for reasons of political vindictiveness, the Highlanders were permitted to distill only on a domestic scale. The modern distilling industry began after the Duke of Gordon proposed more accommodating legislation. One of his tenants, already working outside the law, was the first to apply for a new licence, in 1824. This enterprising character was from a family variously known by the Scottish name Gow and the English-sounding Smith. It has over the years been thought that the family had supported Bonnie Prince Charlie, but recent research suggests that this was not the case. George Smith founded the distillery that became The Glenlivet. His son John Gordon Smith assisted and succeeded him.

After distilling on two other sites nearby, the Smiths moved in 1858 to the present location. In 1880, the exclusive designation "The Glenlivet" was granted in a test case. The company remained independent until 1935 and was acquired by Seagram in 1977.

Not far from the hamlet of Glenlivet, the distillery stands at a point where the grassy valley is already beginning to steepen toward the mountains. Some original buildings remain, and the offices occupy a handsome 1920s house.

Far from its mountain home, and helped by the marketing power of Seagram, The Glenlivet has become the biggest-selling single malt in the large American market.

These pictures, dating from the mid 1920s, show the fermenting vessels above, the stills top right and filling of barrels right, at Glenlivet. Much of the equipment is the same today.

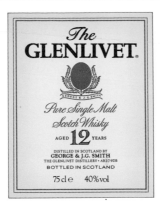

THE GLENLIVET, 12-year-old, 40 vol

Colour Pale gold.

Nose Remarkably flowery, clean and soft.

Body Light to medium, firm, smooth.

Palate Flowery, peachy, notes of vanilla, delicate balance between sweetness and malty dryness.

Finish Restrained, long, gently warming.

SCORE 85

THE GLENLIVET, 21-year-old, 43 vol

Colour Full amber.

Nose Emphatic sherry character.

Body Soft, medium.

Palate At first, very sherryish indeed, with an oloroso character. As the palate develops, that flowery-spicy note becomes strongly evident.

Finish Again, lots of sherry.

SCORE 88

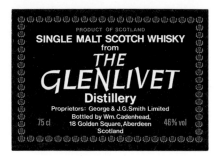

GLENLIVET, 14-year-old, 46 vol, Cadenhead (cask sample)

Colour Pale gold.

Nose Flowery, fruity.

Body Soft, medium.

Palate Peachy, sweet.

Finish Soothing.

SCORE 86

GLENLIVET, 15-year-old, 40 vol, Gordon and MacPhail

Colour Full gold.

Nose Lovely balance of flowery softness and a hint of sherry.

Body Firm, slightly oily.

Palate A little more assertiveness, with some gingery, spicy, notes.

Finish Smooth, aromatic, long-lasting.

SCORE 86

GLENLIVET, 21-year-old, 40 vol, Gordon and MacPhail (cask sample)

Colour Full gold.

Nose Earthy, sherryish (fino or amontillado?)

Body Soft.

Palate Sherryish, with flowery-spicy balance eventually emerging. A dash of herbal, leafy, peaty smokiness.

Finish Smooth, long-lasting.

SCORE 87

GLENLIVET, 24-year-old, 46 vol, Cadenhead (cask sample)

Colour Ripe apple.

Nose Powerful sherry, but the whisky's characteristic peachiness comes through.

Body Soft, medium.

Palate Intense sherry, and some smokiness.

Finish Sherry and smoke, with some astringency. Very long.

SCORE 76

GLENLIVET 1961, 40 vol, Gordon and MacPhail (cask sample)

Colour Very full gold.

Nose Well balanced, fragrant, complex, with some smokiness.

Body Soft.

Palate Sherryish, with long flavour development and some smokiness.

Finish Big, long, warming.

SCORE 88

GLENLOCHY

Distillery rating ☆☆   **Producer** United Distillers
Region Highlands   **District** Western Highlands

THE LOCHY IS A RIVER that passes through Fort William, at the foot of the mountain Ben Nevis. The town of Fort William has two distilleries. One, called Ben Nevis, is in operation; the other, Glenlochy, is not. Glenlochy was built in the 1890s, and was at first water-powered. It changed little over the decades, passed to the Distillers Company Limited in 1953, lost its railway spur in the 1970s, and was closed in 1983. It has been partly dismantled, and seems unlikely to reopen. Its whisky, a good example of a peaty, firm-bodied, Western Highlands malt, is available only in independent bottlings.

GLENLOCHY 1974, 40 vol, Gordon and MacPhail
A malt in which to be wrapped at bedtime.

Colour Full gold.

Nose Light, dry, smoky, peaty.

Body Light to medium, firm oily.

Palate Light at first, dry, becoming oily, developing toward peaty notes.

Finish Peaty, powerful, but over quite quickly.

SCORE 70

GLENLOCHY 27-year-old, 46 vol, Cadenhead (cask sample)

Colour Pale gold.

Nose Light, dry, grassy.

Body Light, firm.

Palate Light, oily.

Finish Quick.

SCORE 69

GLENLOSSIE

Distillery rating ☆☆☆　**Producer** United Distillers
Region Highlands　**District** Speyside (Lossie)

SANDALWOOD, PRIVET? Both have been nosed in this aromatic malt, now available as a single. The distillery, in the valley of the Lossie, south of Elgin, was built in 1876, reconstructed 20 years later, and extended in 1962. Its memorabilia includes a horse-drawn fire-engine: whisky is so combustible that every distillery has had a fire at some time. Next door is the Mannochmore distillery, built in 1971, closed briefly in the 1980s, but now producing again. Mannochmore's malt has never been available as a single.

GLENLOSSIE 10-year-old, 43 vol (cask sample)
Colour Fino sherry.
Nose Fresh. Grass, heather, sandalwood.
Body Light to medium. Soft, smooth.
Palate Malty, dryish at first, developing a complex of sweeter, perfumy, spicy notes.
Finish Spicy.

SCORE 76

Other versions of Glenlossie

A Gordon and MacPhail 1971, 40 vol, is sherryish, but still with plenty of distillery character. SCORE 76. A Scotch Malt Whisky Society 1981, 65.3 vol, was somewhere between the two. SCORE 76.

GLEN MHOR

Distillery rating ☆☆   **Producer** United Distillers
Region Highlands   **District** Speyside (Inverness)

A N UNUSUAL MALT, with its sweet, nutty, character. Try it with fruit cake or apple pie, as a mid-afternoon or holiday treat. Its home city of Inverness, at the western fringe of Speyside, had three malt distilleries – none of which survives. All were owned by The Distillers Company Limited, which became United Distillers. Glen Mhor and Glen Albyn were neighbours on the western side of the city. Glen Mhor, built in 1892, was once powered by a water turbine. For some time, it provided whisky for the Mackinlay blends. It closed in 1983 and has since been demolished, but its whisky can still be found. Purists pronounce it Glen Vawr.

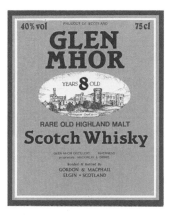

GLEN MHOR Eight-year-old, 40 vol, Gordon and MacPhail

Colour Gold.

Nose "Sweet shop" aroma; treacle toffee?

Body Light, soft.

Palate Sweetly nutty, with some burnt caramel, dryness.

Finish Light, aromatic, surprisingly refreshing.

SCORE 64

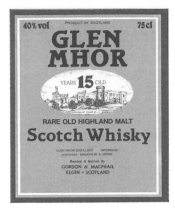

GLEN MHOR 15-year-old, 40 vol, Gordon and MacPhail (cask sample)

Colour Amber.

Nose Sweet, oloroso sherry.

Body Light, soft, smooth.

Palate Enjoyable combination of sherry character and nutty spirit.

Finish Soft, smooth.

SCORE 66

GLEN MHOR 1965, 56.4 vol, Signatory

Colour Reddish-amber. Bright.

Nose Sherry. Drier, but still that "sweet shop" note.

Body Very soft and voluptuous.

Palate Sherry, nuts, treacle toffee. Very distinctive.

Finish Treacle toffee, with some oaky notes.

SCORE 76

GLENMORANGIE

Distillery rating ☆☆☆☆   **Producer** Macdonald & Muir
Region Highlands   **District** Northern Highlands

T HE BIGGEST SELLING SINGLE MALT in Scotland, but from a small company. Glenmorangie (the Scots pronounce it to rhyme with "orangey") made an early start: it has been available as a single since the 1920s. It is an easy taste to embrace – a fairly light, sweetish, flowery, spicy, malt, in which a French perfume house reported finding 26 fragrances, from almond, bergamot and cinnamon to verbena, vanilla and wild mint.

The water flows through sandstone and is hard. The country-side is rich in heather and clover. Lightly-peated malt is used, and a house yeast that imparts an estery, fruity, note. The stills are the tallest in Scotland, at 5.13m (16ft, 10¼in), and probably contribute a delicacy to the spirit. A very narrow cut is taken.

The character of the principal version, a 10-year-old, is also shaped by the exclusive use of Bourbon wood in ageing. The same wood is used in the maturation of the single-cask version first released in 1900. This product is rather fussily identified as "The Native Ross-shire Glenmorangie". The distillery, at Tain, is in the county of Ross-shire. All of its whisky is, of course, native to that county.

While a distillery normally marries many casks of its whisky to make a bottling of single malt, The Native Ross-shire is taken from just one. Each batch comprises fewer than 250 bottles. No two casks of whisky ever have quite the same character, and that will be reflected in this series. Every vintage, labelled with the dates of production and bottling, will be different. They are being bottled at cask strength, so they will even vary slightly in alcohol content. In 1990, Glenmorangie also released an 18-year-old, with some maturation in sherry wood. There have also been older, vintage-dated editions with some sherry ageing which are even spicier, with suggestions of marzipan and aniseed.

Whichever wood is used, the Glenmorangie malts also gain a dimension of character from the coastal location of the distillery. Not only is there the faintest hint of seaweed in the malt, its maturation is also smoothened by the relatively narrow band of temperatures on the coast.

All of Glenmorangie's output is now bottled as a single malt, and the distillery is unusual in that respect. It has been owned since 1918 by Macdonald and Muir, who are also the proprietors of Glen Moray.

GLENMORANGIE 10-year-old, 40 vol

Colour Pale gold.

Nose Spicy (cinnamon, walnut, sandalwood?), with some flowery sweetness, fresh, a whiff of the sea, enticing.

Body On the light side of medium, but with some viscosity.

Palate Spicy, flowery and malty-sweet tones that are creamy, almost buttery.

Finish Long and rounded.

SCORE 80

The Native Ross-Shire Glenmorangie 10-year-old, 57.6 vol
(Distilled 15 May, 1980. Bottled 5 September, 1990.)

Colour Just slightly fuller than the 40 vol.

Nose Deeper, sweeter, spicy.

Body On the heavy side of medium, and very viscous.

Palate Malty-sweet start, then butterscotch, walnut, sandalwood. Lots of flavour development. A splash of water brings out some peaty dryness.

Finish Long, spicy.

SCORE 80

GLENMORANGIE 18-year-old, 43 vol

Colour Full reddish-amber.

Nose Sherry, mint, walnuts, sappy, oaky.

Body Medium, smooth, fleshier.

Palate Sherryish and sweet at first, more walnuts, then the whole pot pourri of spiciness.

Finish Aromatic, nutty, lightly oaky.

SCORE 80

GLEN MORAY

Distillery rating ☆☆☆ **Producer** Macdonald & Muir
Region Highlands **District** Speyside (Lossie)

IT IS PURELY COINCIDENCE that malt whiskies with similar names, Glens Morangie and Moray, are made by the two distilleries of the Macdonald and Muir company. Glen Morangie may be better known, but its more southerly sibling is gaining its own reputation. The principal version of Glen Moray has in recent years been sub-titled '93, to mark the year of Macdonald and Muir's foundation a century ago, though the whisky in the bottles is a mere 12 years old. The bottles are packaged in a series of handsome tins, decorated with the livery of various Highland regiments. There is also a series of vintage-dated bottlings at around 25 years. These have proven very popular.

It is a second coincidence that both Glenmorangie and Glen Moray were formerly breweries. Moray was converted into a distillery in 1897, acquired by Macdonald and Muir in the 1920s, and extended in 1958.

GLEN MORAY 12-year-old, 40 vol
Perhaps a little austere for some, but elegant and well-balanced.

Colour Very pale gold.

Nose Big, rounded, fresh, grassy, new-mown hay, barley notes.

Body Light but smooth and firm.

Palate Ripe, fat, barley.

Finish Fresh, leafy, oatmeal dryness.

SCORE 75

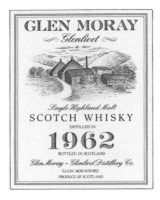

GLEN MORAY 1962 (bottled in 1987), 40 vol

Colour Full gold.

Nose Much sweeter.

Body Smooth, softer.

Palate More maltiness, and more Bourbon character.
Sweeter at first, developing to dryness and a hint of peat.

Finish Big, dry, warming.

SCORE 77

GLEN MORAY 21-year-old, 46 vol, Cadenhead (cask sample)

Colour Full gold.

Nose Grassy.

Body Smooth, soft.

Palate Sweet at first, becoming grassy and lemony.

Finish Big, dry.

SCORE 76

GLEN ORD

Distillery rating ☆☆☆   **Producer** United Distillers
Region Highlands   **District** Northern Highlands

AN IMPORTANT COMPONENT of the Dewar's blends, and an underrated malt as a single. It has impeded its reputation by constantly changing its name. The distillery itself has variously been identified as Muir of Ord, Glen Ord, or simply Ord. In official bottlings, the single malt was for a time known as Glenordie. It has now reverted to Glen Ord. Never mind that the distillery is hardly in a glen; no reasonable malt-lover would wish to encourage any further changes of identity. As compared with the most recent Glenordie, the new Glen Ord has slightly more sherry character.

The distillery is at the village called Muir of Ord, on the neck of the Black Isle, an isthmus between the Moray, Beauly and Cromarty Firths, not far from Inverness. The "Isle" is noted for the cultivation of barley for malting. There is a maltings, with its open-sided peat-barns visible from the road, at the distillery. Muir of Ord was founded in 1838, and modernised in 1966.

GLEN ORD 12-year-old, 40 vol

Colour Amber.

Nose Rounded, with a dash of sherry, sweet and dry malt notes, and a hint of peatiness.

Body Medium to full, soft.

Palate Light touch of sherry. Malty and clean all the way through. Begins simply with the taste of malt. Then comes a dash of barley-sugar sweetness (and a spicy, gingery, note?), followed by a restrained, malty dryness (a hint of peat, too?). Very well balanced.

Finish Dry, gingery, spicy, smooth.

SCORE 75

GLENORDIE 12-year-old, 40 vol

Colour Full, gold.

Nose Profound, with sweet and dry malt notes and a hint of peatiness.

Body Medium to full, very smooth.

Palate Malty, very clean, accented toward sweetness, but with a balancing dryness. So easy to drink, yet full of taste.

Finish Dry, gingery, spicy, smooth.

SCORE 75

ORD 24-year-old, 46 vol, Cadenhead

Colour Bronze.

Nose Deep and dry, with a hint of peat.

Body Medium to full, very smooth.

Palate Malty, with a peaty dryness quickly emerging.

Finish Peaty, very long, some sherry notes.
A 25-year-old version seems to be very slightly fuller all round.

SCORE 77

GLEN ROTHES

Distillery rating ☆☆☆☆   **Producer** Highland Distillers
Region Highlands   **District** Speyside (Rothes)

T HE VENERABLE WINE AND SPIRIT merchants Berry Brothers and Rudd, of St. James's, London (where they trace their origins to the 1690s), have in their blended Scotch whisky Cutty Sark long used a proportion of Glen Rothes. Now, they are marketing Glen Rothes as a bottled single malt, by arrangement with the distillery's proprietors. Berry Brothers and Rudd also independently bottle a number of other malts, but with a discretion that borders on invisibility.

Glen Rothes has long been prized by blenders, and will surely be more widely appreciated as a single malt now that the distillery's owners have entered into this marketing arrangement. It had previously been on sale only when independent bottlings were made. A Gordon and MacPhail eight-year-old was outstanding for its age, and a sherryish 1956 a delight.

The distillery is one of five tucked along the tiny main street of Rothes. Glen Rothes was built in 1878, and enlarged in 1963 and 1980.

GLEN ROTHES 12-year-old (no age statement), 43 vol
Colour Full golden.
Nose Some sherry, very soft fruity-spicy (Box of dates? Dried apricots? Peach skins?), a hint of perfumy smokiness. Appetizing.
Body Medium, silky-smooth.
Palate Caressing, lightly malty, with the faintest hints of sherry, raisins, licorice. Very complex. Opens up with a dash of water.
Finish Spicy, smooth, becoming dry.

SCORE 81

GLEN SCOTIA

Distillery rating ☆☆☆☆   **Producer** Gibson International
Region Campbeltown

C AMPBELTOWN IS TOO EASILY overlooked as a malt region. It still produces extraordinarily distinctive singles, even if there are only three, from a mere two distilleries. The sea-mist character of the region is at its freshest and most startling in Glen Scotia, and not altogether absent from its softer, maltier, vatted partner Royal Culross. These products should not be totally overshadowed by the depth and complexity of their local rivals Springbank and Longrow.

The Glen Scotia distillery, founded around 1832, is in a cottage-like building in a quiet street. It is said to be haunted by the ghost of a former proprietor who drowned himself in Campbeltown Loch after being tricked out of a large sum of money. After a period of closure in the mid 1980s, the distillery reopened toward the end of that decade. With the Lowland distillery Littlemill, it was in the late 1980s backed by the Canadian whisky company Gibson. The name was retained after a management buy-out of Littlemill and Glen Scotia.

GLEN SCOTIA Eight-year-old, 40 vol
Colour Full gold.
Nose Briny, fresh, aromatic, big.
Body Seems light as it meets the tongue, but quickly rounds out to become medium – almost tactile – and smooth.
Palate Very salty and immediately arousing to the appetite.
Finish Remarkably long and powerful.

SCORE 85

GLEN SPEY

Distillery rating ☆☆☆ **Producer** Justerini and Brooks
Region Highlands **District** Speyside (Rothes)

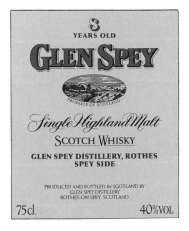

G LEN SPEY BELONGS to the same family as the more familiar Knockando and The Singleton of Auchroisk, and the lesser-known Strathmill. All are owned by Justerini and Brooks, the "J. & B." of blended whisky renown. The original Justerini, from Bologna, Italy, was a distiller and wine merchant. Justerini and Brooks, founded in 1749, is a wine merchant's in St. James's, London. It has for many years been part of the British and worldwide group International Distillers and Vintners (I.D.V.), which also includes Gilbey's Gin and Smirnoff Vodka.

The Glen Spey distillery was founded in 1884 and acquired at a very early stage, in 1887, by Gilbey's. The distillery was completely rebuilt in 1970. Its whisky contributes to blends like Spey Royal and the vatted malt Strathspey, but has in recent years also been marketed on a limited scale as a single malt.

GLEN SPEY Eight-year-old, 40 vol
Colour Gold.
Nose Light, fragrant.
Body On the light side of medium.
Palate Aromatic, faint hints of peat, grassiness and nuttiness.
Finish Light, dryish.
SCORE 73

GLENTAUCHERS

Distillery rating ☆☆ **Producer** Allied Distillers
Region Highlands **District** Speyside

PURE MALT SCOTCH WHISKY
from
GLENTAUCHERS
Distillery
Proprietors: James Buchanan & Co. Ltd.
75 cl — Bottled by Wm. Cadenhead, 18 Golden Square, Aberdeen Scotland — 46% vol

CLOSER TO THE SPEY than to the river Isla, somewhere between the two, this distillery was founded in 1898, extensively remodelled in the 1920s, and rebuilt in 1965. It temporarily closed in the mid 1980s but was then acquired and reopened by Allied Distillers at the end of the decade. In the past, it was one of the distilleries linked with the Buchanan blends. Its malt has been bottled as a single by various independents, most recently Gordon and MacPhail.

GLENTAUCHERS 17-year-old, (distilled 1965, bottled 1982) 46 vol, Cadenhead

Colour Pale, "white wine".

Nose Light, with both malty sweetness and fruity, or perhaps clove-like, phenolic, dryness.

Body Light but smooth.

Palate Seems light at first but becomes quite powerful. Malty, but again with its distinctive dryness.

Finish Very dry, long, warming.

SCORE 71

GLENTAUCHERS 1979, 40 vol, Gordon and MacPhail (cask sample)

Colour "White wine".

Nose Light, dry, faintly phenolic. Old books? Oak. Fino sherry.

Body Light, smooth.

Palate Again, seems light at first, but gradually builds maltiness, power, and that distinctive dryness.

Finish Very dry, almost quinine-like, very warming.

SCORE 71

GLENTURRET

Distillery rating ☆☆☆☆   **Producer** Highland Distillers
Region Highlands   **District** Midlands

A CLAIMANT TO BEING THE OLDEST distillery in Scotland (see also Littlemill and Strathisla), it is without question one of the smallest; producing single malts of a very high quality, in a wide range of ages and proofs.

There are records of a distillery in the neighbourhood at least as early as 1717, and some of the buildings on the present site date from 1775. The distillery itself was dismantled in the 1920s, then revived in 1959 by a noted whisky enthusiast, James Fairlie. His objective was to preserve malt-distilling on a craft scale, in a way that could be seen and appreciated by visitors. The Fairlie family still runs the distillery, though it was acquired in 1981 by Cointreau. The French liqueur company, along with Remy-Martin Cognac, subsequently established links with Highland Distilleries. As a result, Glenturret passed to Highland Distilleries in 1990.

The distillery is on the banks of the river Turret, near Crieff, in Perthshire. It is tucked away in a steep valley between fields and tree-covered hillsides. In the days of illegal distilling, this would have been a good hiding place. Today it retains its rusticity while also being a tourist attraction.

GLENTURRET Eight-year-old, 40 vol

Colour Pale, "fino sherry".

Nose Sweet, malty, fresh.

Body Light but smooth.

Palate Malty, creamy.

Finish Surprisingly long, and very lively.

SCORE 76

GLENTURRET 10-year-old, 57.1 vol (100 proof)

Colour Bright "white wine".

Nose Very appetizing toffeeish maltiness.

Body Big, soft.

Palate Toffee, roasty notes, very powerful.

Finish Nutty, almost juicy.

| SCORE 77 |

GLENTURRET 12-year-old, 40 vol

Colour Full gold.

Nose Malty but rounded, with perhaps a hint of Bourbon wood.

Body Light but smooth.

Palate Malty, nutty, hint of vanilla.

Finish Smooth, long.

| SCORE 74 |

GLENTURRET 5,000 days old, 40 vol

Colour Full gold.	

Nose Sweet, with a little more depth.

Body Light to medium, smooth.

Palate Very tasty. Some raisiny notes, and a good, creamy maltiness.

Finish Long.

SCORE 75

GLENTURRET 15-year-old, 40 vol
A lovely balance of the components in this luscious malt.

Colour Full gold.

Nose Profound, with malty and oaky notes.

Body Medium, chewy.

Palate Malty, roasty, perfumy.

Finish Creamy, smooth, glowing.

SCORE 81

GLENTURRET 15-year-old, 50 vol (87.5 proof; cask strength)
This version achieves a remarkable balance of the whisky's natural character, rich oakiness, and high alcohol.

Colour Full gold.

Nose Malt, walnuts, sherry, oak.

Body Medium, becoming full.

Palate Cream, walnuts, oak – very big flavour development.

Finish Immense.

SCORE 86

GLENTURRET 1972, 43 vol

Colour Full gold, with some depth.

Nose Profound, with malt, nuttiness and some sherry.

Body Medium, rounded.

Palate Very complex, with all the components beautifully dovetailed.

Finish Nutty, rich, powerful.

SCORE 90

GLENTURRET 1967, 50 vol

This huge malt is a delight for lovers of heavily-sherried whiskies. Given its vintage in combination with its proof, it may well have more intensity of sherry character than any other malt.

Colour Deep amber-red.

Nose Rich sherry aroma.

Body Full, slightly liqueurish, but by no means overbearing.

Palate Very sherry-accented.

Finish Soft, rich, warming, long.

SCORE 86

GLENTURRET 1966, 40 vol

Colour Full gold, with amber tinges.

Nose Profound, with dry oloroso sherry arising from its depths.

Body Medium to full, soft.

Palate Very complex and dovetailed, with nuttiness emerging at length.

Finish Very smooth, nutty, perfumy, long.

SCORE 91

GLENUGIE

Distillery rating ☆☆   **Producer** Whitbread (Long John)
Region Highlands   **District** Eastern Highlands

CONNOISSEURS CHOICE

Connoisseurs Choice, a range of single malts from various districts of Scotland.

In the Highlands are situated the greatest number of malt whisky distilleries.

SINGLE HIGHLAND MALT SCOTCH WHISKY
DISTILLED AT
GLENUGIE
DISTILLERY
PROPRIETORS: Long John Distillers Ltd

DISTILLED **1966** DISTILLED

SPECIALLY SELECTED, PRODUCED AND BOTTLED BY
75cl   **GORDON & MACPHAIL**   40%vol
ELGIN · SCOTLAND
PRODUCT OF SCOTLAND

T HIS ASSERTIVE MALT has never been "officially" bottled as a single, though it is still available from merchants. Glenugie has plenty of character, but the elements are not well combined or balanced. The supply is finite, since the distillery closed in 1982, and the equipment has been dismantled.

The river Ugie flows into the sea at the port and boat-building·town of Peterhead, and the distillery site is nearby, close to the vestiges of an old fishing village. There was first a distillery on the site in the 1830s, but this was converted into a brewery, and the present buildings date from 1875. The distillery was last operated by the Whitbread brewing company, at that time under its Long John subsidiary. The distillery buildings still stand, but have been sold to companies outside the drinks industry.

GLENUGIE 1966, 54.8 vol, Gordon and MacPhail (cask sample)

Colour Bright gold.

Nose Ripe fruitiness. Fino sherry? Some phenolic smokiness.

Body Soft, medium, malty, smooth, with some syrupiness.

Palate Powerful, with honeyish sweetness at first, becoming gingery, with some slightly sulphury sherry notes. Becomes considerably sweeter when water is added.

Finish Assertive, dry.

SCORE 70

GLENURY ROYAL

Distillery rating ☆☆☆   **Producer** United Distillers
Region Highlands   **District** Eastern Highlands

G LENURY ROYAL IS ON THE EAST COAST, south of Aberdeen, and close to the fishing port and resort of Stonehaven. The distillery takes its name from the glen running through the Ury district. Its founder, Captain Robert Barclay, a local Member of Parliament, was also an athlete and marathon walker. This flamboyant character had a friend at court to whom he referred coyly as "Mrs Windsor", and through whose influence he was given permission by King William IV to style his whisky "Royal". The distillery was founded in 1825 and rebuilt in 1966. Its whisky – a good, straightforward, Highland malt – can be found as a bottled single malt, though it has never been widely available, nor very well known. It has an uncompromisingly dry, smoky, style. Despite its fairly light body, it has plenty of palate. It is a component of the blends made by the small company John Gillon, a Distillers Company Limited subsidiary until the takeover by United Distillers. The distillery has been temporarily closed since 1985.

GLENURY ROYAL 12-year-old, 40 vol

Colour Bronze.
Nose Aromatic, dry, smoky.
Body Light to medium, firm.
Palate Toasty, dry, maltiness, developing toward smokiness.
Finish Smoky, with a hint of buttery, honeyish, sweetness. Very long.

SCORE 76

GLENURY ROYAL 13-year-old, 46 vol, Cadenhead (cask sample)

Colour Pale gold.

Nose Sherryish, despite the colour. Dry. Aromatic.

Body Light, slightly oily.

Palate Sweetish, toasty, becoming dry. Hints of fino sherry?

Finish Hints of honey, warming.

SCORE 75

GLENURY ROYAL 22-year-old, 46 vol, Cadenhead (cask sample)

Colour Amber-red.

Nose Sherryish (oloroso?), aromatic, appetizing.

Body Light to medium, soft.

Palate Sherryish start, with lots of oloroso character, developing toward some smokiness.

Finish Sherry, smokiness, well-rounded and satisfying.

SCORE 77

HIGHLAND PARK

Distillery rating ☆☆☆☆☆ **Producer** Highland Distilleries
Region Highlands (Island) **District** Orkney

THE GREATEST ALL-ROUNDER in the world of malt whisky. Definitely in an island style, but combining beautifully all the elements of a classic single malt: smokiness (with its own heather-honey accent); maltiness; smoothness; depth, roundness and fullness of flavour; length of finish (though perhaps not at its youngest). Lovely any time, and splendid as a nightcap. As a single malt, Highland Park develops to great ages. In blends, Highland Park is said to be a catalyst, bringing out the flavours of the other contributing malts.

The distillery is near Kirkwall, capital of the Orkneys. Highland Park, the northernmost of Scotland's distilleries, is said to have been founded in the 1790s. The distillery has its own floor maltings. A well-peated malt is used. The peat is dug locally, from shallow beds that provide a "young", rooty, heathery, character. Some maltsters traditionally tried to achieve this character by throwing heather onto the fire. The smokiness in Highland Park does seem to vary slightly.

**HIGHLAND PARK Eight-year-old, 40 vol, Gordon and MacPhail
(cask sample)**

Colour Rich gold.

Nose Smoky and heathery, light.

Body Medium.

Palate Fresh, smoky, leafy, sappy, with buttery notes.

Finish Honeyish, but rather quick.

SCORE 85

HIGHLAND PARK 12-year-old, 40 vol

Colour Amber.

Nose Smoky, "garden bonfire" sweetness, heathery, malty, hint of sherry.

Body Medium, exceptionally smooth.

Palate Succulent, with smoky dryness, heather-honey sweetness and maltiness.

Finish Teasing, heathery, delicious.

> SCORE 90

HIGHLAND PARK 24-year-old, 46 vol, Cadenhead
Although neither the colour nor the nose suggests much sherry (until water is added), the palate does.

Colour Gold.

Nose Deeper, rounder, drier.

Body Medium.

Palate Heather-honey still, but again deeper, rounder and drier, with some sherry.

Finish Dry, slightly woody, long.

> SCORE 87

IMPERIAL

Distillery rating ☆☆☆   **Producer** Allied Distillers
Region Highlands   **District** Speyside

A POWERFUL, OLD-FASHIONED Highland malt that can be found only in independent bottlings. Perfect for bedtime. The distillery is in Carron, just across the river from Dailuaine, with which it was historically linked. Imperial was founded in 1897, and extended in 1965. It closed briefly in the mid 1980s, then was reopened by Allied.

IMPERIAL 1970, 40 vol, Gordon and MacPhail

Colour Full, gold.

Nose Sherryish, aromatic, smoky.

Body Medium to full, soft, rich.

Palate Malty, with notes of barley and vanilla, smoky, and full of flavour. A powerful, interesting, combination of malty sweetness and peaty smokiness.

Finish Soft, smoky.

SCORE 76

IMPERIAL 1979, 40 vol, Gordon and MacPhail (cask sample)

Colour Very pale gold.

Nose Some vanilla-like malty sweetness, but sharp at back of nose.

Body Medium to full at first, but drying on the tongue.

Palate Vanilla, chocolate, hints of fruit, becoming sharp.

Finish More chocolate, then warming and alcoholic.

SCORE 75

INCHGOWER

Distillery rating ☆☆☆   **Producer** United Distillers
Region Highlands   **District** Speyside

SPEYSIDE
SINGLE MALT
SCOTCH WHISKY

The *Oyster Catcher* is a common *sight*
around the

INCHGOWER

distillery, which stands *close* to the *sea*
on the mouth of the *RIVER SPEY*
near *BUCKIE*. *Inchgower*,
established in 1824, produces *one* of the
most *distinctive single* malt whiskies
in *SPEYSIDE*. It is a malt for the
discerning drinker ~ a *complex* aroma
precedes a *fruity, spicy*
taste ⚜ with a hint of *salt*.

A G E D **14** Y E A R S

43% vol   Distilled & Bottled in SCOTLAND. INCHGOWER DISTILLERY, Buckie, Banffshire, Scotland   70 cl

I N CHARACTER, LESS OF A Speyside malt (though the distillery is near the mouth of that river) than a coastal one. Inchgower is near the fishing town of Buckie. To the palate expecting a more flowery, elegant, Speyside malt, this one can seem assertive, or even astringent, in its saltiness. With familiarity, that can become addictive. A lovely, sustaining, dram after a stroll by the sea or a day's fishing. An earlier 12-year-old was slightly sweeter, and fractionally more sherryish, than the newer 14, which has more distillery character.

The enterprise has its origins in 1825, but the Inchgower distillery was built in 1871, and expanded in 1966. It was at one stage briefly owned by the town council.

INCHGOWER 14-year-old, 43 vol (cask sample)

Colour Pale gold.

Nose An almost chocolatey spiciness; then sweet notes like edible seaweed; and finally a whiff of saltier sea character. Overall, dry and complex.

Body Light to medium. Smooth.

Palate Starts sweet and malt, with lots of flavour developing, eventually becoming drier and salty.

Finish Very salty, lingering appetizingly on the tongue.

SCORE 76

INCHMURRIN

Distillery rating ☆☆ **Producer** William Morton
Region Highlands **District** Western Highlands

INCHMURRIN IS A MONASTIC ISLAND in Loch Lomond. Just south of the loch, albeit in surroundings that owe more to industrial archaeology, the single malt of the same name is made. The distillery is called Loch Lomond, and it has a second malt, Old Rhosdhu. Loch Lomond is able to make more than one malt because its pot stills are of an unusual design, and can produce whiskies of different weights.

INCHMURRIN, no age statement, 40 vol

Colour Full amber (darker than previous, 12-year-old, version).

Nose Eucalyptus?

Body Medium.

Palate Smooth, pleasantly oily. Very long flavour development. Eucalyptus. Very unusual.

Finish Soothing, warming. After a dip in Loch Lomond?

SCORE 67

OLD RHOSDHU, no age statement, 40 vol

Colour Amber.

Nose Scented. A luxurious malt to drink in the bath?

Body Light.

Palate Dry, perfumy, spicy.

Finish Wintergreen? Perhaps not the bath – the sauna.

SCORE 65

INVERLEVEN

Distillery rating ☆☆ **Producer** Allied Distillers
Region Lowlands **District** West

A VERY RARE MALT, produced in the imposing distillery complex at Ballantine's home base in Dumbarton. For many years, this complex operated two pot-still houses to produce malt whisky for the Ballantine blends. Each produced a different malt whisky, and the two were known internally as Inverleven and Lomond. Neither malt has ever been officially released as a single, but Inverleven can be found in independent bottlings. In recent years, the Inverleven stills have been de-commissioned, and all malt produced at Dumbarton comes from the Lomond system. This system, which has a passing resemblance to a brandy alembic, generally produces a heavier, oilier spirit. In addition to these whiskies, and those from the company's distilleries elsewhere in Scotland, a very wide range of other malts go into the soft but complex Ballantine blends. Further bottlings of Inverleven are expected from Gordon and MacPhail.

The edifice of the Ballantines cluster of distilleries, towers above the river Leven, which gives its name to a rare malt.

INVERLEVEN 17-year-old (Distilled 1966, Bottled 1984), 46 vol, Cadenhead

Colour Gold.

Nose Dry, delicate, perfumy, grassy, hint of smoke, cedarwood, nectarine?

Body Seems light at first, but becomes fuller and rounder.

Palate Gingery, crisp.

Finish Fruity, powerful.

SCORE 67

INVERLEVEN 21-year-old 46 vol, Cadenhead (cask sample)

Colour Pale, greeny-gold.

Nose Perfumy, grassy, hint of nectarine?

Body Seems light at first, but is very well rounded.

Palate Orangey, gingery.

Finish Expressive, orangey, appetizing.

SCORE 69

JURA

Distillery rating ☆☆☆ **Producer** Invergordon
Region Highlands (Island) **District** Jura

IN THE INNER HEBRIDES, close to Islay, the isle of Jura is inhabited by 225 people (George Orwell was briefly a resident) and rather more deer. It is also noted for two mountain peaks known as the Paps (breasts) of Jura, and one malt distillery.

The distillery seems to have been founded around 1810, and was rebuilt in 1876. Though a couple of buildings dating back to its early days are still in use, the present distillery was built during the late 1950s and early 1960s, and enlarged in the 1970s. It was owned for a time by Scottish and Newcastle Breweries, and its malt whisky is an important component of the Mackinlay blends.

Lightly peated malt is used, and the water flows primarily over rock. The stills have very high necks, producing a light, relatively clean, spirit, with only a slight island character. Bottlings of the single in greater ages are planned.

The famous Paps, or mountains, of the island of Jura seen from across the Sound of Islay.

ISLE OF JURA 10-year-old, 40 vol

Colour Golden.

Nose Hint of sherry, albeit light and dry. Some buttery maltiness. A faint hint of peat when water is added.

Body Light, soft.

Palate Sweetish, slowly developing a faint hint of island dryness and saltiness.

Finish A little malt and some saltiness.

SCORE 71

JURA 20-year-old, 46 vol, Cadenhead

Colour Amber-red.

Nose Pronounced sherry, with lots of depth.

Body Beautifully smooth.

Palate Sherry and, even through it, much more pronounced island character.

Finish Dry, salty.

SCORE 76

KINCLAITH

Distillery rating ☆☆ **Producer** Whitbread (Long John)
Region Lowlands **District** West

KINCLAITH WAS THE LAST malt distillery in the city of Glasgow. It was built in 1957, to become part of a complex that already housed the Strathclyde grain distillery. The original owners were the American company Schenley, through their subsidiaries Seager Evans and Long John. When the latter was sold to Whitbread, in 1975, Kinclaith was dismantled to make room for an extension to the grain distillery.

The independent bottlers still have stocks of Kinclaith. The Gordon and MacPhail bottlings reveal a soft, seductive, malt, perhaps helped along by a little sherry. The Cadenhead version is much drier.

CONNOISSEURS CHOICE

Connoisseurs Choice, a range of single malts from various districts of Scotland.

The lowlands traditionally produce smooth soft and mellow whiskies.

SINGLE LOWLAND
MALT SCOTCH WHISKY
DISTILLED AT
KINCLAITH
DISTILLERY
PROPRIETORS: Long John Distillers Ltd
DISTILLED **1967** DISTILLED
SPECIALLY SELECTED, PRODUCED AND BOTTLED BY
75cl **GORDON & MACPHAIL** 40%vol
ELGIN · SCOTLAND
PRODUCT OF SCOTLAND

KINCLAITH 1967, 40 vol, Gordon and MacPhail (cask sample)
Colour Amber.
Nose Smoky, some sherry, faintly sulphury.
Body Light, delicate.
Palate Light, soft, restrained, fruitiness. Melon?
Finish Soothing, tasty. Melon. Sherry.

$$\boxed{\text{SCORE 68}}$$

PURE MALT SCOTCH WHISKY
from
KINCLAITH
Distillery

Proprietors: Long John Distilleries Ltd.

75 cl   Bottled by Wm. Cadenhead,   46% vol
18 Golden Square, Aberdeen
Scotland

KINCLAITH 20-year-old, 46 vol, Cadenhead

Colour Very pale.

Nose Smoky, phenolic.

Body Light, soft.

Palate Light, gingery. A light, aromatic, aperitif, dryness.

Finish Light, dry.

SCORE 65

CONNOISSEURS
CHOICE

Connoisseurs Choice, a
range of single malts from
various districts of
Scotland.

The lowlands
traditionally produce
smooth soft and mellow
whiskies.

SINGLE LOWLAND
MALT SCOTCH WHISKY
DISTILLED AT
KINCLAITH
DISTILLERY
PROPRIETORS: Long John Distillers Ltd

DISTILLED 1966 DISTILLED

SPECIALLY SELECTED PRODUCED AND BOTTLED BY
75cl   GORDON & MACPHAIL   40%vol
ELGIN · SCOTLAND
PRODUCT OF SCOTLAND

KINCLAITH 1966, 40 vol, Gordon and MacPhail

Colour Bronze.

Nose Smoky.

Body Light, very soft.

Palate Lightly fruity (melon dusted with ginger?).

Finish Soft, tasty, melon-like.

SCORE 69

KNOCKANDO

Distillery rating ☆☆☆   **Producer** International Distillers
Region Highlands   **District** Speyside

KNOCKANDO IS THE FLAGSHIP distillery of I.D.V./ Justerini and Brooks and produces a malt whisky of some elegance. The whisky is marketed as a single malt under its season of distillation; the year of bottling is also indicated on the label. The notion is that the whisky is bottled when it is mature, rather than at a specific age.

The age range of vintages offered has varied from 10 to 15 years. As the object is to produce a consistently mature malt, one vintage does not vary dramatically from another. Even with a gap of some years, there was little difference between the 1974 and '77, for example. Perhaps the 1977 was fractionally softer on the nose and lighter and drier in palate, but it is hard to be sure. The Extra Old Reserve may have become slightly more sherryish between 1964 and 1965. The soubriquet indicates a separate series of vintages, again doubly dated, and with a greater depth of character all round.

KNOCKANDO 1975 (bottled 1990), 43 vol
Colour Pale gold.
Nose Fragrant, perfumy.
Body Light but notably smooth.
Palate Soft, fresh, but with a depth of flowery, nutty, faintly minty, sweetness.
Finish Soft, sweet, but very clean. Flowery, fragrant, lightly smoky notes. Becoming drier.

SCORE 76

KNOCKANDO Extra Old Reserve, 1965 (bottled 1990), 43 vol
Presented in a square decanter with a wired top.

Colour Gold.

Nose Fuller and more rounded. Some sherry?

Body Light to medium.

Palate A little more malty sweetness, perhaps a faint hint of oakiness, and more depth. Soft, mellow, elegant, beautifully balanced.

Finish A little more smokiness.

> **SCORE 77**

KNOCKDHU

Distillery rating ☆☆☆ **Producer** Knockdhu Distillery Co
Region Highlands **District** Speyside

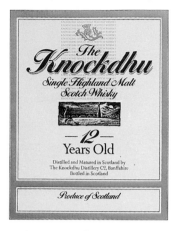

THE WELCOME FIRST OFFICIAL bottling of this enjoyable and interesting malt was in 1990, almost a century after the distillery's foundation. The distillery is in the village of Knock, between the rivers Spey, Isla and Deveron. It was the first to be established by the Distillers Company Limited, and was used to provide malt whisky for the blenders Haig. In 1983 it was closed, but five years later it was acquired, and subsequently reopened, by the partners in Inver House, under the name of the Knockdhu Distillery Company. Knockdhu was the first of the many distilleries to reopen toward the end of the decade and in the early 1990s.

KNOCKDHU 12-year-old, 40 vol
Colour Gold, with tinges of bronze.
Nose Very aromatic, but soft. Cream, vanilla, pineapple?
Body Light to medium. Firm.
Palate Crisp, clean, dry, fruitiness. Pineapple? Seville orange?
Finish Dry, aromatic, faintly herbal.

SCORE 74

Other versions of Knockdhu
A 15-year-old (43 vol), tasted as a cask sample, was drier on the nose, but much more rounded in body and finish. SCORE 75.

LADYBURN

Distillery rating ☆☆ **Producer** William Grant and Sons
Region Lowlands **District** West

PURE MALT SCOTCH WHISKY
from
LADYBURN
Distillery
Proprietors: William Grant & Sons Ltd.
Bottled by Wm. Cadenhead,
75 cl   18 Golden Square, Aberdeen   46% vol
Scotland

GLENFIDDICH'S LOWLAND PARTNER and, like Glenfiddich, a component of the Grant's blended whiskies. Unlike Glenfiddich, however, Ladyburn was not really intended for consumption as a single malt. Ladyburn is a very well-made Lowland malt, but it is a whisky made to be blended. It has a certain fresh-faced charm, but has no pretensions to depth of character. As a single malt, it is available only from independent bottlers. In some of their older vintages, it has a degree of Bourbon-wood character, but this is not especially noticeable in the most up-to-date examples. Ladyburn was a modern distillery, opened in 1966, but it had a short life. The distillery was closed in the mid 1970s. An adjoining grain distillery, Girvan, remains.

LADYBURN 20-year-old, 46 vol, Cadenhead

Colour Very pale, "white wine".

Nose Light, fruity, dry.

Body Light, soft.

Palate Light, medium-sweet, quickly becoming perfumy and dry.

Finish Powerful, dry.

SCORE 57

LAGAVULIN

Distillery rating ☆☆☆☆☆ **Producer** United Distillers
Region Islay **District** South shore

THE CLASSIC ISLAY WHISKY, with the driest start of any single malt. More instantly assertive than even its immediate (and rightly exalted) neighbours, Ardbeg and Laphroaig, it also has a more sustained power and a greater complexity. Intensely dry, from its pungent bouquet to its astonishing long finish.

Its attack is reminiscent of Lapsang Souchong tea, but supported by a big, malty, sweetish (Darjeeling this time?), background. The third generous element is sherry. A big, immensely sophisticated, whisky. Some devotees feel that the dryness is better expressed in the 12-year-old, which was the principal version until it was largely replaced by the 16-year-old. Others feel that the greater sherry character of the 16-year-old makes for a more complete symphony.

Decanter magazine compared the relationship of Lagavulin and Laphroaig on Islay with that of Cheval Blanc and Petrus in Bordeaux. In name at least, Lagavulin must be the Cheval Blanc as it contributes malt whisky to the White Horse blends, and the animal decorates the distillery sign. At a glance, the cream-painted distillery buildings could be an inn called The White Horse. The distillery's water arrives by way of a fast-flowing stream that no doubt picks up plenty of peat on the way. The maturation warehouses are battered by the sea, and have their own jetty.

Lagavulin (pronouced "Lagga-voolin") means "the hollow where the mill is". There are reputed to have been 10 illicit stills on this bay in the mid 1700s. There were certainly two distilleries here in the early 1800s, and they combined in the 1830s.

When the seas are high, Lagavulin's outer walls are knee-high in salt water.

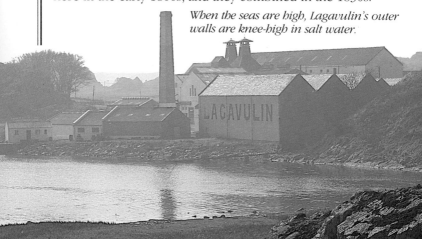

LAGAVULIN 12-year-old, 43 vol

Colour Pale amber.

Nose Sea-salt, peat, intense dryness, sherry.

Body Full, round, syrupy.

Palate Dry, smoky, peaty, salty.

Finish Salty, dry, smoky, a roaring crescendo. Complex and immense.

SCORE 89

LAGAVULIN 16-year-old, 43 vol
At its best neat.

Colour Full amber.

Nose More sherry.

Body Full, smooth.

Palate The dryness of the whisky itself is at first offset by the sweetness of the sherry character. As the palate develops, the salty notes in particular emerge.

Finish Huge, powerful, peaty, salty, embracing.

SCORE 95

LAPHROAIG

Distillery rating ☆☆☆☆　　**Producer** Allied Distillers
Region Islay　　**District** South shore

L OVE IT OR HATE IT, Laphroaig's distinctiveness is too much for even some hardened malt-lovers. The medicinal character is addictive to some devotees, but an impenetrable barrier to the faint-hearted. Like hospital gauze, said one taster. Medicinal, reminiscent of mouthwash or disinfectant, phenolic, tar-like? That is the whole point: the iodine-like, seaweed character of Islay. The famous Laphroaig attack has diminished a little in recent years, unmasking more of the sweetness of the malt, but it is still a very characterful whisky, with a distinctively oily body.

Laphroaig has its own peat-beds on Islay, and a beautifully-maintained floor maltings at the distillery. Its maturation warehouses face directly on to the sea.

The distillery was built in the 1820s by the Johnston family, whose name is still on the label. In 1847 the founder died after falling into a vat of partially-made whisky. There were no doubt more raised eyebrows when, in the late 1950s and early 1960s, the distillery was owned by a woman, Miss Bessie Williamson.

LAPHROAIG®

**SINGLE ISLAY MALT
SCOTCH WHISKY**

10
Years Old

**The most richly flavoured of
all Scotch whiskies**

**ESTABLISHED
1815**

DISTILLED AND BOTTLED IN SCOTLAND BY

D. JOHNSTON & CO. (LAPHROAIG), LAPHROAIG DISTILLERY, ISLE OF ISLAY.

75cl ℮　　　　　　43%vol

LAPHROAIG 10-year-old, 43 vol

Colour Full, refractive, gold.

Nose Medicinal, phenolic, seaweedy, with a hint of sherry.

Body Medium, oily.

Palate Seaweedy, salty, oily.

Finish Round and very dry.

SCORE 86

LAPHROAIG®

SINGLE ISLAY MALT
SCOTCH WHISKY

15 *Years Old*

The most richly flavoured of
all Scotch whiskies

75cl e ESTABLISHED **1815** 43% Vol

Prodotto ed imbottigliato in Scozia da
D.JOHNSTON & CO.(LAPHROAIG), LAPHROAIG DISTILLERY,
ISLE OF ISLAY.
Importato da F. & C. S.p.A.-TORINO
Lic. UTIF No.386-TORINO

LAPHROAIG 15-year-old, 43 vol

Colour Pale amber.

Nose Drier, deeper.

Body Medium to full, with a soothing oiliness.

Palate A deceptive moment of sherryish sweetness, then a burst of Islay intensity.

Finish Round, dry, long, warming.

> SCORE 89

LAPHROAIG 16-year-old, 57 vol, Cadenhead (cask sample)

Colour Pale gold.

Nose Very dry, with a faint hint of sherry.

Body Full, very oily.

Palate Powerful, sweet at first, then salty and dry.

Finish Oily, salty, warming.

> SCORE 81

LAPHROAIG 1974, 55 vol, Signatory (cask sample)

Colour Deep amber-red, almost tawny.

Nose Intense seaweed. Slightly sour.

Body Medium to full, drying on tongue.

Palate Intense, sweet, sherry, edible seaweed, phenolic. High points for character, but lacks balance.

Finish Dry, very late seaweed, warming.

> SCORE 87

LINKWOOD

Distillery rating ☆☆☆☆   **Producer** United Distillers
Region Highlands   **District** Speyside (Lossie)

OSE-WATER? MARZIPAN? Romantic tasting-notes are evoked by this perfumy, malty, Speyside classic. It has an elegance and complexity beloved of devotees, though it has never hit the heights of fashion. This malt has traditionally been bottled with a definite sherry accent. The sherry ageing seemed to complement the perfumy sweetness of the whisky. A new version has no obvious sherry character, so that the whisky itself shines through. As always, there will be differing views on this. The new version, in United Distillers "flora and fauna" series, is arguably more assertively character-ful, but less complete.

Linkwood is on the Lossie, close to Elgin. It was founded in the 1820s, and rebuilt in 1872, 1962 and 1971. That last extension effectively made it into two distilleries, "old" and "new". Despite its growth, it has a traditionalist outlook. Whisky-writer Philip Morrice recalls that at one stage the management forbade even the removal of spiders' webs in case a change in the environment should affect the whisky.

LINKWOOD 12-year-old, 40 vol

Colour	Full, gold.
Nose	Sweet, light-but-definite sherry character, and some depth.
Body	Medium, rounded.
Palate	Sweet start, developing to lightly smoky dryness.
Finish	Dryish, smooth, confident, lots of finesse.

SCORE 83

LINKWOOD 12-year-old, 43 vol ("Flora and fauna")

Colour Very pale, "white wine".

Nose Remarkably flowery. The rose-water without the sherry. Fragrant. Clean and sweet.

Body Medium, rounded, slightly syrupy.

Palate Starts slowly, and has a long sustained development to its full, rosy, fresh, sweetness. One to savour.

Finish Perfumy, faintly smoky, long.

SCORE 82

LINKWOOD 15-year-old, 40 vol, Gordon and MacPhail

Colour Amber.

Nose Sweet, sherryish, deep.

Body Medium.

Palate Sweet, not at all cloying, beautifully rounded.

Finish Dries out slightly. Clean, and deliciously smooth.

SCORE 85

LINKWOOD 18-year-old, 46 vol, Cadenhead (cask sample)
For lovers of sherry-aged malts, this is a most interesting example.

Colour Dark amber.

Nose Powerful sherry character.

Body Full, smooth.

Palate Rich, sherryish, with whisky's own character firmly underpinning.

Finish Intense, rich sherryish.

SCORE 85

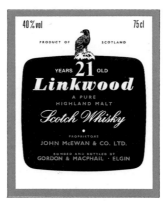

LINKWOOD 21-year-old, 40 vol, Gordon and MacPhail (cask sample)

Colour Amber-red.

Nose Marzipan, rosewater, ginger?

Body Medium to full.

Palate Aromatic, sweet and rounded.

Finish Soft, sherryish, soothing.

SCORE 86

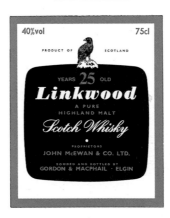

LINKWOOD 25-year-old, 40 vol, Gordon and MacPhail

Colour Amber-red.

Nose Sherryish.

Body Medium to full.

Palate Complex. Very long flavour development. Some of the sweetness has rounded out with age.

Finish Softly dry, deep and very long.

SCORE 87

LITTLEMILL

Distillery rating ☆☆☆☆ **Producer** Gibson International
Region Lowlands **District** North west

A CLASSIC LOWLAND MALT, from a distillery that may be the oldest in Scotland. Among the several claimants to the greatest antiquity, Littlemill cites the earliest specific date for its foundation, 1772. The first clear records of its ownership, however, date from 1817. It was rebuilt in 1875, though its overgrown, cottage-like, buildings look older. Triple distillation was used until the 1930s. Across the road from the distillery is an early mechanised maltings.

The site, at Bowling, is between Glasgow and Dumbarton. The distillery closed for a year or so in the late 1980s, but reopened in 1988/9. The Lowland style is to produce single malts that are light in taste, gentle, soft, sweet and fresh. Littlemill's is a wholehearted example. The full freshness is best experienced in the eight-year-old "official" bottling. The Cadenhead version, at 22-years-old, has more roundness and depth but less freshness and softness.

LITTLEMILL Eight-year-old, 43 vol
Colour Very pale, "white wine".
Nose Marshmallow? Perhaps toasted marshmallows.
Body Light to medium, soft.
Palate Deliciously malty-sweet, yet somehow not overbearing. Marshmallow again, perhaps powdery icing sugar?
Finish Very smooth, slight dryness. Coconut?

SCORE 83

PRODUCT OF SCOTLAND
SINGLE MALT SCOTCH WHISKY
from
LITTLEMILL
Distillery
Proprietors: Littlemill Distillery Co. Ltd.

75 cl   Bottled by Wm. Cadenhead,
18 Golden Square, Aberdeen   46% vol
Scotland

LITTLEMILL 22-year-old, cask strength, Cadenhead (cask sample)

Colour Pale gold.

Nose Drier, deeper, more aromatic.

Body Light to medium, well rounded.

Palate Sweet but beautifully-rounded.

Finish Oily, coconut-like.

SCORE 83

LOCHNAGAR

Distillery rating ☆☆☆☆   **Producer** United Distillers
Region Highlands   **District** Eastern Highlands

Q UEEN VICTORIA IS REPUTED to have enjoyed this malt, and to have used it to lace her claret, thereby ruining two of the world's greatest drinks. She visited the distillery, which is at the foot of the mountain of Lochnager (1156m/3,789ft) and very close to the Royal family's Scottish home at Balmoral.

A man believed originally to have been an illicit whisky-maker established the first legal Lochnagar distillery in 1826, and the present premises were built in 1845. Three years later, the Royal family acquired Balmoral. The then owner recorded that he wrote a note inviting Prince Albert to come, and was rewarded with a visit the very next day. Soon afterwards, the distillery began to supply the Queen, and became known as Royal Lochnagar. Over the years, the distillery has been rebuilt three times, most recently in 1967. For a period in the late 1970s and early 1980s, the distillery stopped using the "royal" prefix, but this has now been restored.

The single malt is well-rounded, dry and urbane. In 1988/9, a "super-premium" bottling from selected casks, and with a greater degree of sherry ageing, was introduced. This Selected Reserve, first went on sale in duty-free shops, at a price of £55 ($75-$80).

With its "Royal" prefix restored and the release of its Selected Reserve Malt this is becoming a justifiably better-known distillery.

LOCHNAGAR 12-year-old, 40 vol

Colour Full, gold.

Nose Big, with some smokiness.

Body Medium to full. Smooth.

Palate Light smokiness, restrained fruitiness and malty sweetness.

Finish Again, dry smokiness and malty sweetness. The first impression is of dryness, then comes the sweet, malty counter-point.

SCORE 80

LOCHNAGAR Selected Reserve, no age statement, 43 vol

Colour Amber-red.

Nose Lots of sherry. Slight sulphur note.

Body Big, smooth.

Palate Lots of sherry, malty sweetness, and plenty of smokiness.

Finish Smoky.

SCORE 83

LOCHSIDE

Distillery rating ☆☆☆   **Producer** Macnab Distilleries
Region Highlands   **District** Eastern Highlands

O NCE THE WELL-KNOWN James Deuchar brewery, Lochside has been a distillery since 1957. The premises are on a filled-in loch, hence the name. Lochside is in Montrose. Since 1973 the distillery has been in Spanish ownership, and much of its malt goes into the Distilieras y Crienza blended whisky, a major product in Spain. In Scotland, there is also a good splash of Lochside in the Sandy Macnab's blend.

LOCHSIDE 10-year old, 40 vol
Colour Gold.
Nose Some flowering currant.
Body Light to medium, soft, smooth.
Palate Malty start, but not especially sweet. Lots of flavour development. Fruity (blackcurrant?). Becoming dry.
Finish Gentle, not very long.

SCORE 74

Other versions of Lochside
Gordon and MacPhail 1966 (40 vol), sherryish with sweet finish. SCORE 73. Signatory 1966 (43 vol), drier, slightly oaky. SCORE 71. Signatory 1959 (58.5 vol, casks sample), sherry and oak. SCORE 72.

LONGMORN

Distillery rating ☆☆☆☆ **Producer** Seagram
Region Highlands   **District** Speyside (Lossie)

ONE OF THE GREATEST SPEYSIDE MALTS, but not widely available as a single. In so far as Longmorn can be found at all, the 15-year-old version is most often sighted. Longmorn's malt whisky is prized by blenders at least as highly as those of its sister distilleries Glen Grant and The Glenlivet (pp. 111, 120) though in the market for bottled single malts, it has been given less play than these longer-established and more famous siblings.

Longmorn is a relative youngster, having been conceived in 1894 and born in 1895. It has a disused water-wheel and a workable steam engine. The distillery was extended twice during the 1970s.

Longmorn's malt is appreciated for its great complexity, with its combination of cleanness and fullness of character, from its big bouquet to its long finish. Delightful before dinner, though some tasters would save it until after dessert.

LONGMORN 12-year-old, 40 vol
Colour Full, bright, gold.
Nose Complex, firm.
Body Firm, smooth, gentle.
Palate Deliciously fresh, cereal grain maltiness. Slow, long, flavour development, evolving toward a clean, flowery, fruitiness.
Finish Clean, smooth, appetizing. Surely this one is a pre-dinner malt.

SCORE 85

LONGMORN 15-year-old, 43 vol

Colour Full, gold.

Nose Big, slightly oily, barley malt, flowery notes.

Body Smooth, rounded, medium to big.

Palate Very emphatic, fresh, clean, cereal grain maltiness.

Finish Clean, malty but dry, nutty, hint of sherry, appetizing, very long.

SCORE 87

LONGMORN 24-year-old, cask strength, Cadenhead (cask sample)

Colour Gold.

Nose Big, cereal grain, flowering currant.

Body Big, rich.

Palate Much sweeter, with emphatic sherry notes.

Finish Powerful, very long.

SCORE 85

LONGMORN 1962, 40 vol, Gordon and MacPhail (cask sample)

Colour Full amber.

Nose Very sherryish.

Body Big, round.

Palate Extremely sherryish, but still with some distillery character.

Finish Sherryish, big, warming.

SCORE 86

LONGMORN 1960, 40 vol, Gordon and MacPhail (cask sample)

Colour Amber.

Nose Sherryish.

Body Big, round.

Palate Extremely sherryish.

Finish Sherryish, warming. Definitely a digestif.

SCORE 85

THE MACALLAN

Distillery rating ☆☆☆☆☆ **Producer** Macallan
Region Highlands **District** Speyside

"T HE ROLLS-ROYCE OF SINGLE MALTS" is a soubriquet often bestowed upon this persistent winner of competitions. From its unusually small stills to its insistence upon sherry ageing (always in dry oloroso casks, shipped unbroken from Spain), Macallan is a purposefully traditionalist distillery. In the big, heavily sherried, style, there is no malt more widely acknowledged than The Macallan. It is the classic example of this type of Speyside whisky.

The sherry ageing, and its consistency, are the trademark of The Macallan. Sceptics argue that the sherry dominates, but that is manifestly not true. There are more heavily-sherried whiskies, but none with the particular profile of The Macallan: its complex of sherry, maltiness, slight smokiness, flowering currant and Calvados-like notes, with its own distinctive dryness, roundness and depth. It is a malt with big, bold, clear tones from aroma to finish. Between those two extremes is a beautifully composed whole.

Even in the seven-year-old, bottled exclusively for the Italian market, this malt is full of flavour. One of The Macallan's several celebrated adherents, the novelist Kingsley Amis, insists that the 10-year-old version is, in his words, "the best glass". There is a considerable development of character between the 10- and the 12-year-old while many devotees prefer the 18-year-old. The whisky writer Wallace Milroy proposed the 1964 vintage as the stuff of legend. A rival case, so to speak, might be made for the 1950, with its slightly oily, peaty, palate and spectacularly long finish. There have been a number of special editions. A limited edition of an oaky 60-year-old, with a label by the artist Peter Blake, fetched £6,000 for one bottle.

There has probably been whisky made on the Macallan site, on a small hill overlooking the Spey near Craigellachie, since the late 1700s. A farmer on the hillside first made whisky there from his own barley. A manor house from this period has been restored as a place at which to entertain private visitors. An illustration of the house is used on the box that accommodates each bottle of The Macallan. It is intended to convey the sense of a whisky "Château", and perhaps to offset the harder lines of what is a functional-looking distillery.

The first licenced distillation at Macallan is said to have taken place in the earliest days of legalised production, in 1824. In

1892 the business came into the hands of the family who still manage Macallan and have a major share in the company.

Macallan went public in 1966-8, and was thus able to finance the laying down of large stocks of whisky for maturation, and a decade of expansion. Each extension involved the building of a new still-house, so that the company could increase production without altering the size of its stills.

The company was already renowned among blenders, who use its malt whisky as a "top dressing", but in the 1960s Macallan as a bottled single malt was available only on Speyside. Although the larger share of the malt continues to be reserved for blending, a new generation of family management decided to market seriously a bottled single. The Macallan, stressing the definite article, was launched nationally in Britain in 1980. Like other pioneers of singles, Macallan has tried to limit independent bottlings. There is nonetheless one well-known example, quaintly labelled "As We Get It", and marketed by J.G. Thomson, the spirits and wine subsidiary of Bass in Scotland.

The launch of The Macallan was steered to success by the present chairman, Allan Schiach, a member of the family, and a successful screenwriter.

MACALLAN Seven-year-old, 40 vol (cask sample)
(Italian market only.)

Colour Bright amber.	
Nose Sherry, with dry maltiness in background.	
Body Medium to full.	
Palate Sherryish and sweetish, with malt and fruit coming up behind.	
Finish Satisfying, sherryish, malty-buttery. A light digestif.	

SCORE 81

THE MACALLAN 10-year-old, 40 vol

Colour Amber.

Nose Sherry, and buttery, honeyish, malt character. Lots of roundness and depth, even at this young age.

Body Full, without being syrupy.

Palate Lots of sherry, without being rich. Plenty of malt. Sweetish.

Finish Satisfying, malty, gingery, becoming dry, with a hint of smoke.

SCORE 87

THE MACALLAN 10-year-old, 57 vol (100 proof)

Colour Amber, marginally fuller.

Nose Sherry, still, but drier. A soft whiff of alcohol.

Body Full.

Palate Sherryish. A very clean, rounded, fruitness. Intense. Powerful.

Finish Sherry, smoke, alcohol.

SCORE 89

THE MACALLAN 12-year-old, 43 vol

Colour Amber.

Nose Sherry, honey, flowery notes.

Body Full, smooth.

Palate The first hints of flowering currant. Altogether more expressive.

Finish Slightly more rounded.

SCORE 91

THE MACALLAN 18-year-old, 43 vol, distilled 1973, bottled 1991

Colour Full amber.

Nose Much more assertive sherry character. Very perfumy.

Body Full, round.

Palate More complexity and fullness of flavour, with flowering currant and Calvados-like notes.

Finish Slow at first, then oaky, sappy, and powerful.

SCORE 94

THE MACALLAN 25-year-old, 43 vol

Colour Full amber-red.

Nose Definite smokiness overlaying the characteristics.

Body Full, firm, round.

Palate The smokiness greatly enhances the complexity.

Finish Dry, complex, very long.

SCORE 95

THE MACALLAN "As We Get It", no age statement, 57.2 vol, J.G. Thomson

Colour Amber.

Nose Powerful, with both sherry and buttery-malty notes.

Body Full.

Palate For a moment, sweet, then quickly becoming dry and spirity.

Finish Assertive.

SCORE 84

MILLBURN

Distillery rating ☆☆☆　**Producer** United Distillers
Region Highlands　**District** Speyside (Inverness)

AS THE NIGHT TRAIN from London finishes its 11-hour journey to Inverness, the sleepy-eyed traveller glides by the distillery buildings that once housed Millburn. It is no longer a distillery, having been closed in 1985 and later converted, with scant tribute to its origins, into a pub and steakhouse. There are less appropriate metamorphoses, of course. The city's other two distilleries, Glen Albyn and Glen Mhor, were razed to make room for shops.

Millburn dated at least from the beginning of licensed distilling in the Highlands, and its buildings from 1876, 1898 and 1922. The whisky has never been officially bottled, but has contributed to a vatted malt called The Mill Burn.

MILLBURN 1971, 40 vol, Gordon and MacPhail

Colour Reddish amber.

Nose Rich, aromatic, sherry start, becoming dry.

Body Full, smooth, quite firm.

Palate Sherry, malt, and smokiness, in quick succession. Possibly a fraction sweeter and more aromatic than its predecessor, the 1966.

Finish Smoky, peaty, slowly developing into a long, warming, memory of a robust malt.

SCORE 76

MILTONDUFF

Distillery rating ☆☆☆   **Producer** Allied Distillers
Region Highlands   **District** Speyside (Lossie)

PLUSCARDEN PRIORY, said to have been the first site of the Miltonduff distillery, still exists, and its ruins have been restored. Although there is no present-day connection with the distillery, the name of the Priory is invoked on the box that houses the Milton Duff bottle. The distillery, established in 1824, was extensively modernised in the 1930s and again in the 1970s.

After a period in which the label on the official bottling spelled the name as two words, they have now been united, to match the style used by the distillery itself. Whatever the spelling, Miltonduff is a flowery, clean, firm, elegant malt, produced in quite large stills. It is very well regarded by blenders. For a time, the company also had a Lomond still, producing a heavier malt, which was known as Mosstowie. The still has been dismantled, but the malt can still be found in independent bottlings.

MILTONDUFF 12-year-old, 43 vol

Colour Soft gold.

Nose Fragrant, dry, flowery, with faint hints of peat and vanilla. Peatiness more evident when a little water is added.

Body Medium, firm smooth.

Palate Sweet, very clean and delicately flowery.

Finish Aromatic, soothing, with some malty dryness.

SCORE 76

MILTONDUFF 1963, 40 vol, Gordon and MacPhail

Colour Amber.

Nose Sherryish (fino?).

Body Medium, smooth.

Palate Sherryish, sweet, some vanilla notes.

Finish Powerful, long. Perhaps better after dinner.

SCORE 76

MOSSTOWIE 1975, 40 vol, Gordon and MacPhail

Colour Bronze, reddish.

Nose Very appetizing. Fresh, leafy, smoky, dry.

Body Medium to full, firm, oily.

Palate Full of flavour, with notes of leafiness, smokiness and maltiness.

Finish Flowery but assertive. Hints of smokiness.
A hearty restorative.

SCORE 76

MORTLACH

Distillery rating ☆☆☆☆   **Producer** United Distillers
Region Highlands   **District** Speyside (Dufftown)

A HEARTY WELCOME to the first truly "official" bottling, a 16-year-old in United Distillers' "flora and fauna" series. Mortlach heartily embraces all the pleasures of a good Speyside single malt: smokiness, maltiness, fruitiness, complexity, sherry character.

The distilling water comes from springs in the Conval Hills, and seems to bring a powerful taste with it (the malt is said to be only lightly peated). The cooling water is from the river Dullan.

There is said to have been an illicit distillery on the site, and the legal one traces its history to 1823. It is very attractive, despite having been modernised in 1903 and 1964. Mortlach was the first legal distillery in Dufftown, now such an important centre for the industry. Its bottled single and those of neighbours Glendullan and Dufftown arguably offer something of a local style in their robust, well-rounded, attack.

SPEYSIDE
SINGLE MALT
SCOTCH WHISKY

MORTLACH

was the first of seven
distilleries in *Dufftown*. In the
19th farm animals kept in
adjoining byres were fed on
barley left over from processing.
Today *water* from springs in
the *CONVAL HILLS* is used to
produce this delightful
smooth, fruity single
MALT SCOTCH WHISKY.

AGED **16** YEARS

Distilled & Bottled in SCOTLAND.
MORTLACH DISTILLERY
Dufftown, Keith, Banffshire, Scotland

43% vol   70 cl

MORTLACH 16-year-old, 43 vol (cask sample)

Colour Profound, rich, amber.

Nose Dry oloroso sherry. Smoky, peaty.

Body Medium to full, firm, smooth.

Palate Sherryish, smoky, peaty, sappy, some fruitiness, assertive.

Finish Long and dry.

SCORE 81

MORTLACH 12-year-old 40 vol, Gordon and MacPhail

Colour Pale amber.

Nose Smoky, malty, profound.

Body Medium to full, rich.

Palate Smokiness, maltiness, fruitiness, in a deliciously expressive balance.

Finish Well-balanced, long, dry, with sherry notes.

SCORE 81

MORTLACH 21-year-old 40 vol, Gordon and MacPhail (cask sample)

Colour Amber.

Nose Sherry. Dry oloroso? Clean, powerful, rich, delicious.

Body Medium to full, rounded.

Palate Sherryish at first, then very smoky. As arousing to the senses as a log fire.

Finish Long, round, dry.

SCORE 81

NORTH PORT

Distillery rating ☆☆ **Producer** United Distillers
Region Highlands **District** Eastern Highlands

THE NAME INDICATES THE NORTH GATE of the once-walled small city of Brechin. The distillery was built in 1820. The pioneering whisky writer Alfed Barnard, who toured Scotland's distilleries in the 1880s, recorded that this one obtained its barley from the farmers around Brechin, its peat and water from the Grampian mountains. The present-day whisky historian Derek Cooper, reports that the condensers were cooled in a stream that ran through the distillery. North Port was modernised in the 1970s, and closed in 1983. Its whisky can still be found as a single malt from the independent bottlers. The whisky has also been a component of the Glen Dew vatted malt and the Heather Dew blends.

NORTH PORT 1970, 40 vol, Gordon and MacPhail
Colour Full gold.
Nose Dry, astringent. The addition of water brings out smoky and sherryish notes.
Body Light to medium, but seems quickly to collapse and become watery.
Palate Sweetish and malty at first, becoming dry, with hints of peat-smoke. The addition of water rounds out the taste, and makes for quite a pleasant malt.
Finish Very dry.

SCORE 64

OBAN

Distillery rating ☆☆☆☆   **Producer** United Distillers
Region Highlands   **District** Western Highlands

IF THE WESTERN HIGHLANDS has a capital, it is the town of Oban. If the region has a classic malt, it is the one that bears the town's name. The mainland of the Western Highlands does not have many distilleries, but in general its whiskies tend to be well-rounded and malty, with some smokiness. These are after-dinner malts, but the meal should have been hearty – venison, perhaps?

This is still a thinly-populated part of Scotland. The first settlers arrived by sea and came to this coast in 5,000 BC, making their homes in caves in the cliffside. That story, and a later account of Scottish invasion from Antrim in Ireland, are told on the label of the 14-year-old Oban, in The Classic Malts series offered by United Distillers. This version is replacing the 12-year-old, which was put into a bottle that looked as though it contained perfume.

The traveller returning from the islands of Mull or Iona, or from Fingal's Cave, sees Oban as a Victorian town, with the distillery growing out of those cliffside caves. The distillery is said to have been founded in 1794, though the present buildings probably date from the 1880s. The stillhouse was rebuilt in the late 1960s and early 1970s, and there was further work in 1991. The Oban malt whisky has contributed to the various John Hopkins blends, including one romantically called Old Mull.

"The gateway to the Isles", the ferry town of Oban, has a distillery producing a malt with a definite coast and island character.

OBAN 12-year-old, 43 vol

Colour Amber.

Nose "Pebbles on the beach", said one taster. Certainly a whiff of the sea, but also a touch of fresh peat, and some maltiness.

Body Medium to full, smooth, firm.

Palate Smooth, malty, fruity, developing a smoky dryness.

Finish Sweetish, gingery, warming.

SCORE 76

OBAN 14-year-old, 43 vol

Colour Amber.

Nose More assertive all round, especially in peaty smokiness.

Body Quite rich, smooth, slightly viscous.

Palate Dry, smoky, with malty and fruity undertones.

Finish Aromatic, smooth.

SCORE 79

PITTYVAICH

Distillery rating ☆☆ **Producer** United Distillers
Region Highlands **District** Speyside (Dufftown)

ONE OF THE NEWEST DISTILLERIES, built by Bell's in 1975 as a partner to next-door neighbour Dufftown. In the late 1980s, enthusiasts for single malts began to wonder whether the product would become available to them. Then independent bottler James MacArthur released a 12-year-old revealing the perfumy "soft pear" house character. The same bottler has since added a 14-year-old which more assertively pronounces its dry finish. A bottling of the same age from the Scotch Malt Whisky Society was similar, but seemed to have more spicy dryness on the nose. None of these bore obvious signs of sherry ageing. In 1991 there was finally an official bottling, at 12 years old, in United's "flora and fauna" series. This has all of the other characteristics, plus a hefty dose of sherry. In any form, this is an assertive malt, and it will be too astringent for some drinkers. Its breadth of character is released only with a generous splash of water.

PITTYVAICH 12-year-old, 43 vol (cask sample)
Colour Deep amber-red.
Nose Sherryish, perfumy, pear-skin.
Body Medium.
Palate Very sherryish. Assertive. Some malty chewiness. Soft, sweet, pear-like fruitiness, moving to a spicy dryness.
Finish Spicy, perfumy, intensely dry, lingering.

SCORE 69

PORT ELLEN

Distillery rating ☆☆☆☆ **Producer** United Distillers
Region Islay **District** South Shore

THE RAREST OF ISLAY MALTS. The distillery, founded in the 1820s and expanded in the 1960s, was temporarily closed in 1984, and is still held in reserve by United. The distillery's white-painted warehouses form an attractive "street" close to the sea in Port Ellen, one of the three principal villages on Islay. Port Ellen is also one of the two ferry terminals on the island.

Adjoining the distillery is a modern maltings, issuing pungent peat smoke lest anyone requires reminding of the island's preoccupation. The malt goes to two other Islay distilleries owned by United Distillers: Lagavulin and Caol Ila.

PORT ELLEN 1971, 40 vol, Gordon and MacPhail

Colour Amber.

Nose Powerful seaweed, saltiness, peppery notes, spicy, grassy. Wonderfully aromatic and arousing to the senses.

Body Medium.

Palate A dash of sherry softens the attack, but still a dry malt, with salt and pepper to the fore. Perhaps more sherryish, and peppery, and less oily, than the 1970.

Finish Extraordinarily peppery.

SCORE 79

PULTENEY

Distillery rating ☆☆☆   **Producer** Allied Distillers
Region Highlands   **District** Northern Highlands

KNOWN AS "THE MANZANILLA OF THE NORTH", for its salty tang. The producers of Manzanilla do supply casks to the Scotch whisky industry, and it is certainly possible that the odd butt has accommodated a charge of Pulteney whisky, but in general the owners are more inclined towards Bourbon wood. The saltiness probably owes more to the sea air. Not only is the Pulteney distillery on the coast, its site is so exposed as to be falling off the furthest end of Scotland. It is the northernmost distillery on the mainland, at Wick.

Pulteney was founded in 1826 and rebuilt by the Hiram Walker company in 1959, as a contributor of malt whisky to the Ballantine blends. Its bottled single, a natural pre-dinner malt, is known as Old Pulteney.

OLD PULTENEY Eight-year-old, 40 vol, Gordon and MacPhail
Colour Amber.
Nose Fresh, dry, with a hint of sea air.
Body Light, firm.
Palate Faintly salty, earthy-spicy, appetizing, smooth, becoming gently malty.
Finish Salty, tangy, warming, soothing, long.
SCORE 77

ROSEBANK

Distillery rating ☆☆☆☆   **Producer** United Distillers
Region Lowland   **District** Central

THE CLASSIC LOWLAND MALT in the view of some devotees, though the competition has hotted up in recent years with the wider availability of rivals like Glenkinchie, Bladnoch, Auchentoshan and Littlemill.

In true Lowland tradition, Rosebank is triple-distilled, and that may contribute to its clean dryness. The 12-year-old version scores for Lowland softness, though the original character of the whisky is most evident in the less sherryish 15-year-old, which is quite popular in the Italian market. The appropriately flowery Rosebank malt whiskies are a component in the George IV blends.

Rosebank is at Cemelon, Falkirk, on the Forth-Clyde canal, between Edinburgh and Glasgow. The distillery's origins may be as early as 1817. Its history begins to emerge more clearly in the 1840s, and some buildings from the 1850s and 1860s survive, straddling the main road.

ROSEBANK Eight-year-old, 40 vol

Colour Amber.

Nose Dry, grassy-flowery, pot pourri aroma. Dryish hint of sherry.

Body Light, but very smooth.

Palate Dry, flowery, fruity. Becomes much less dry when water is added.

Finish Dry.

SCORE 76

ROSEBANK 12-year-old, 43 vol (cask sample)

Colour Gold. This new "flora and fauna" 12-year-old is clearly less sherried than the earlier, Distillers' Agency, bottling.

Nose Grassy-flowery (clover?), light, dry.

Body Light, smooth, slightly syrupy.

Palate At first a malty, sweetish, floweriness. Stays flowery, but becomes gingery and dry.

Finish Again grassy and flowery, but crisp (almost sharp) and dry.

SCORE 77

ROSEBANK 15-year-old, 50 vol

Colour Gold.

Nose Flowery.

Body Surprisingly soft.

Palate Light, sweetish, flowery, clean fruitiness. Very appetizing.

Finish Big, soft, long.

SCORE 77

ST MAGDALENE

Distillery rating ☆☆ **Producer** United Distillers
Region Lowland **District** Central

CONNOISSEURS CHOICE

Connoisseurs Choice, a range of single malts from various districts of Scotland.

The lowlands traditionally produce smooth soft and mellow whiskies.

SINGLE LOWLAND
MALT SCOTCH WHISKY
DISTILLED AT
ST. MAGDALENE
DISTILLERY
PROPRIETORS : John Hopkins & Co. Ltd
DISTILLED **1965** DISTILLED
SPECIALLY SELECTED, PRODUCED AND BOTTLED BY
GORDON & MACPHAIL
ELGIN · SCOTLAND
PRODUCT OF SCOTLAND
75cl 40%vol

THE NAME DERIVES FROM LAND known as St Magdalene's Cross, but the specific site of the distillery is Linlithgow, an ancient town with a lovely loch and a ruined royal palace, in which Mary Queen of Scots was born. Both the single malt and the distillery have sometimes been identified simply as Linlithgow. The town, which is to the west of Edinburgh, close to the Forth, was once a centre of malt-distilling in the Lowlands.

St Magdalene seems to have been founded in the early 1800s, and became the area's principal malt distillery after a multiple merger in 1914. It closed permanently in 1983.

ST MAGDALENE 1965, 40 vol, Gordon and MacPhail (cask sample)
Colour Amber-red.
Nose Sherry. Very perfumy. Grassy, faintly smoky. Slightly oaky.
Body Light to medium. Soft. Smooth.
Palate More perfumy than the 1964. Less of the "grassy bonfire", but it is still there.
Finish Dry but soft. Warming, gentle.

SCORE 68

SCAPA

Distillery rating ☆☆☆　**Producer** Allied Distillers
Region Highlands (Island)　**District** Orkney

SCAPA FLOW, a stretch of water linking the North Sea to the Atlantic, is famous for its roles in both World Wars. In the First, naval ships in the Flow saved the Scapa distillery from destruction by fire. The distillery is near Kirkwall, on the island the Orcadians call "the mainland". Scapa fails to be the northernmost distillery in Scotland by only half a mile. Scapa makes a single malt with the sharpness of an Orkney breeze, the heatheriness of the islands, and its own distinctively oily, "dark chocolate" character. The distillery was founded in 1885, and was powered by a waterwheel that has now been restored. Two of its original warehouses survive, now used for the storage of empty casks, but most of the rest of the fabric dates from 1959, when Scapa was rebuilt.

The water supply is very peaty, but the distillery uses wholly unpeated malt. It has a Lomond wash-still, and uses Bourbon casks for its bottled single malt.

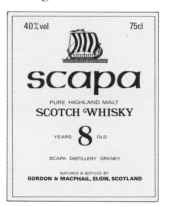

40%vol　　　75cl

scapa

PURE HIGHLAND MALT
SCOTCH WHISKY

YEARS **8** OLD

SCAPA DISTILLERY ORKNEY

MATURED & BOTTLED BY
GORDON & MACPHAIL, ELGIN, SCOTLAND

SCAPA Eight-year-old, 40 vol, Gordon and MacPhail
After a hearty walk before dinner.

Colour Amber.

Nose Fresh, sea-breeze saltiness, new-mown hay, heather, some Bourbon character.

Body Medium, silky.

Palate Salty, slightly sharp, tangy.

Finish Oily but dry, appetizing.

SCORE 76

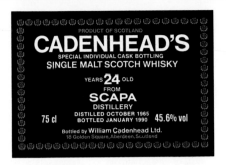

SCAPA 24-year-old, 46.5 vol, Cadenhead
(Distilled 1965. Bottled 1990.)

Colour Gold.

Nose Salty and sharp. Appetizing.

Body Medium, soft, smooth.

Palate Salty, hay-like, heathery, perfumy.

Finish Salty, appetite-arousing.

SCORE 77

SCAPA 1963, 40 vol, Gordon and MacPhail (cask sample)
A nightcap.

Colour Full amber.

Nose Powerful. Wonderfully briny.

Body Medium, soft, smooth.

Palate Salty and sharp, but also with caramelly Bourbon and bitter-chocolate notes.

Finish Bitter-chocolate, long, sustaining.

SCORE 79

SINGLETON

Distillery rating ☆☆☆☆   **Producer** International Distillers
Region Highlands   **District** Speyside

"**A** DESIGNER WHISKY", said the cynics, when The Singleton was launched as a bottled malt in 1986. The brand-name, seeking to imply a singularity, was (and is) contrived, ostensibly because the producers felt that the name of the distillery, Auchroisk (pronounced Othroysk) was too difficult for the prospective consumer.

The Singleton leans toward the full-bodied, well-sherried, style, but with the elegance and finesse rather than voluptuousness. If anything, the most recent vintage was fractionally more sherried and less aromatic, but that cannot be said for certain. Without sherry, the malt is sweet, with a hint of aniseed, as evidenced by a Cadenhead bottling under the Auchroisk label.

The distillery was established by the International Distillers subsidiary Justerini and Brooks. Twelve years passed before the first whisky was released as a bottled single malt.

THE SINGLETON 1978, 40 vol

Colour Full amber.

Nose Emphatic sherry accent.

Body Extraordinarily smooth. Medium-bodied, but almost chewy.

Palate Licorice? Aniseed? Toffee? Then sherryish and fruity.

Finish Liqueur-ish, with a hint of smoke.

SCORE 79

SPEYBURN

Distillery rating ☆☆☆   **Producer** United Distillers
Region Highlands   **District** Speyside (Rothes)

T HERE ARE MANY CLAIMANTS to being the most beautifully situated distillery in Scotland, and Speyburn is surely one of them. This handsome Victorian distillery, set in a deep, sweeping, valley, makes a spectacular sight on the road between Rothes and Elgin. It was built in 1897 and, despite modernisations over the years, has not undergone dramatic change.

Its whisky is not easy to find but a first official bottling, introduced in 1991, makes it a little more accessible.

Set in a hollow in the rolling hills of the Spey valley, the Speyburn distillery produces an all-too-rare characterful malt.

SPEYBURN 12-year-old, 43 vol (cask sample)

Colour Pale gold.

Nose Very dry.

Body Medium, smooth.

Palate Slightly sweet and malty, developing a herbal, heathery dryness.

Finish Dry, warming, aromatic, assertive.

SCORE 71

SPEYBURN 1971, 40 vol, Gordon and MacPhail
Dry enough to drink before dinner, but at its best afterwards.

Colour Bronze.

Nose Dry, heathery, perhaps a hint of sherry.

Body Big, smooth.

Palate Dry maltiness, with heather-honey notes.

Finish Soft, becoming sweeter, rather quick.

SCORE 71

SPEYBURN 22-year-old, cask strength, Cadenhead (cask sample)

Colour Pale gold.

Nose Very dry.

Body Medium, firm, smooth.

Palate Slightly sweet and malty, developing toward hints of dryness.

Finish Dry, warming, satisfying.

SCORE 70

SPRINGBANK

Distillery rating ☆☆☆☆☆ **Producer** J. and A. Mitchell
Region Campbeltown

T HE CLASSIC CAMPBELTOWN MALTS are those produced and matured on the peninsula by the Springbank distillery. The Springbank malts have a briny quality that seems more evident in the Campbeltown whiskies than in those from any other coast. This is married with their characteristic sweetness, and with a great depth.

Springbank has been owned by branches of the same family since it was founded in 1828, and continues to be run with characteristic Scottish caution. Like many distilleries, it has had its periods of closure, and that presumably accounts for the current lack of Springbank at 12 years old. In a tasting held in London by *The Times*, Springbank at 12 years came top, and was rated Premier Grand Cru Classé. That tasting was conducted by wine-writer Jane McQuitty in 1983. More recent bottlings of the 12-year-old have evinced some pear-drop spiritiness, and have not represented Springbank at its most impressive.

The 15- and 21-year-old are now the principal versions. In the case of the 21-year-old, recent bottlings are very heavily sherried, but the house character still eventually fights through. Sensitive souls might flinch at so much sherry and oak, but in offering such mighty malts Springbank wins points for eclecticism and daring. Devotees still remember a wonderful Amontillado cask bottled by the Scotch Malt Whisky Society. A recent adventure was the "West Highland" limited edition: the barley was grown on neighbouring farms and malted at Springbank with local peat. Even the coal that fired the stills came from a local mine, long since closed. The commendably detailed back-label specifies that everything was produced within eight miles, with the "outstanding exception" of the sherry casks.

The Springbank distillery also produces a more heavily-peated whisky called Longrow. This is a splendidly old-fashioned malt of great individual character, almost a classic in its own right. It is not readily recognized as a Campbeltown malt, and has assertive dryness that some tasters find closer to Islay. In *Decanter* magazine, taster Val Brown found Longrow an almost heraldic animal: "The aroma of wet sheep ... the attack of tigers claws". Set round a courtyard, Springbank has three stills, but uses them in conventional, double, configuration. It is an elderly eccentric among distilleries.

SPRINGBANK 15-year-old, 46 vol

Colour Gold.

Nose Briny, fresh, rounding out to a savoury sweetness.

Body Light to medium, smooth, round, sturdy.

Palate A very slight savoury sweetness at first, developing toward the typically briny character.

Finish Again, both the sweetness and saltiness in their own elusive combination. Very warming and extremely long, with a whiff of peat.

SCORE 88

SPRINGBANK 21-year-old, 46 vol

Colour Full amber.

Nose Sherry; nuttiness (coconut?); peat and brine.

Body Medium to full. Soft, slightly chewy.

Palate Sherry, toffee, coconut, edible seaweed, grass, peat brine. Very long flavour development. For such a big malt, suprisingly gentle.

Finish Coconut. Oily. Long.

SCORE 91

SPRINGBANK WEST HIGHLAND 1966, 58.1 vol (cask sample)

Colour Brownish-red, almost mahogany.

Nose Oaky. Heavily sherried. Smoky, but still fragrant, with a hint of (salty?) sharpness.

Body Big, tongue-coating.

Palate Sherry at first; then oak, with sappiness and saltiness emerging somewhere; coconut and then a cough-syrup, soothing, quality.

Finish More sherry, balanced by an oaky dryness, then the cough-syrup again. Very long, soothing and digestif.

SCORE 93

LONGROW 1974, 46 vol (cask sample)

Colour Full gold, with a reddish tinge.

Nose Pungent, earthy, peaty, phenolic.

Body Medium to full, very oily.

Palate Sweeter and more sherryish than some earlier vintages, but still splendidly phenolic and peaty.

Finish Salty, intense, tenacious.

SCORE 90

STRATHISLA

Distillery rating ☆☆☆   **Producer** Seagram (Chivas Brothers)
Region Highland   **District** Speyside (Strathisla)

THE OLDEST DISTILLERY in the north of Scotland. In the 13th century, Dominican monks used a spring nearby to provide water for the brewing of beer. The same water, with a touch of calcium hardness and scarcely any peat character, has been used in the distillation of whisky since at least 1786.

Strathisla, which has also at times been known as Milltown, began its life as a farm distillery. It started to take its present shape from the 1820s onwards, especially after a fire in 1876. In 1950 it was acquired by Seagram.

Lightly-peated malt is used, wooden wash-backs and small stills, two of them coal-fired. Although wooden wash-backs are by no means unusual, Strathisla believes that fermentation characteristics play a very important part in the character of its dry, fruity, oaky, malt whisky. The only official bottling is the 12-year-old, but a range of of ages is bottled under the distillery's name by Gordon and MacPhail.

STRATHISLA Eight-year-old, 40 vol, Gordon and MacPhail

Colour Amber.

Nose Dry, sherryish. Quite complex.

Body Medium, firm.

Palate Dry maltiness, developing to sweeter notes,
with cereal-grain and sherry character.

Finish Big, dry, slightly sappy, lingering.

SCORE 79

STRATHISLA 12-year-old, 40 vol

Colour Full gold.

Nose Dry, sherryish, complex, still with that cereal-grain character.

Body Medium, soft.

Palate Sherryish at first, developing to a dryish malty character. Very well balanced.

Finish Very smooth, long, soothing.

SCORE 79

STRATHISLA 15-year-old, 40 vol, Gordon and MacPhail

Colour Full amber.

Nose Dry, sherryish, complex, still with that cereal-grain character.

Body Medium, quite rich.

Palate Lots of sherry character, though quite dry. Lovely dry oakiness.

Finish Smooth, soothing.

SCORE 80

STRATHISLA 20-year-old, 46 vol, Cadenhead

Colour Rich amber-red. Very dark indeed.

Nose Powerful, sweet, juicy, sherry aroma, but still the oak and the whisky make themselves known underneath all of this.

Body Very rich.

Palate Rich, raisiny, sherry character at first, followed by the oakiness and the spirit itself.

Finish Lots of sherry, and very warming. Earns points for daring to be so heavily-sherried.

SCORE 76

STRATHISLA 21-year-old, 40 vol, Gordon and MacPhail

Colour Full amber.

Nose Sherryish, again with the cereal-grain balance.

Body Medium, smooth.

Palate Sherry-accented, soft.

Finish Sherryish, long, warming.

SCORE 76

STRATHISLA 25-year-old, 40 vol, Gordon and MacPhail

Colour Amber-red.

Nose Very sherryish.

Body Medium, soft.

Palate Sherry-accented, soft.

Finish Sherryish, long, warming. The sherry is beginning to dominate, and the character of the whisky receding.

SCORE 75

STRATHISLA 35-year-old, 40 vol, Gordon and MacPhail

Colour Full gold.

Nose Some welcome smokiness.

Body Soft, smooth.

Palate Light, sweetish.

Finish Light, smooth. Less sherryish than its closest peers, but mellow.

SCORE 75

TALISKER

Distillery rating ☆☆☆☆　**Producer** United Distillers
Region Highlands (Island)　**District** Skye

O NE OF THE MOST INDIVIDUALISTIC of single malts, with a powerful palate and an emphatic island character. What the bigger examples of Zinfandel are to wine, Talisker is to single malts. It has a distinctively peppery character, so hot as to make one taster's temples steam. The phrase 'explodes on the palate' is among the taste descriptions used by blenders at United Distillers. Surely they had Talisker in mind when they composed this phrase. 'The lava of the Cuillins' was another whisky taster's response. The Cuillins are the dramatic hills of Skye, the island home of Talisker. The distillery is on the exposed west coast of the island, on the seaweedy shores of Loch Harport.

After a number of false starts on the other sites, the distillery was established in 1831, and expanded in 1900. For much·of its life, it used triple distillation, and in those days Robert Louis Stevenson ranked Talisker as a style on its own, comparable with the Islay and Glenlivet whiskies. It switched to double distillation in 1928, and was partly rebuilt in 1960, after a fire.

Its eight-year-old bottled single malt has recently begun to be replaced by a 10-year-old, which is featured in the Classic Malts range. Some malt-lovers prefer the dry assertiveness of Talisker at the lesser age, though the older version does have a fuller, more rounded, character.

Talisker is the only distillery on Skye, though the island is also the home of a company making a vatted malt, called Poit Dubh, and a blend, Te Bheag. Both are said to contain some Talisker, and their hearty palates seem to support this suggestion. A dry, perfumy, blended whisky called Isle of Skye is made by the Edinburgh merchants Ian Macleod and Co. The style of whisky liqueur represented by Drambuie is said to have originated on Skye, though that product is now made in Edinburgh, by a family-owned company.

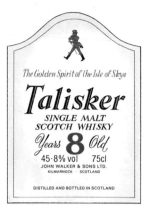

TALISKER Eight-year-old, 45.8 vol

Colour Amber.

Nose Pungent, with smoke, seaweed, brine and sweet maltiness.

Body Medium to full.

Palate Sweet and malty at first, developing a distinctive sourness, then its characteristically peppery notes.

Finish Peppery, hot, powerful. A huge, glowing peat fire that warms the heart for what seems to be hours.

SCORE 89

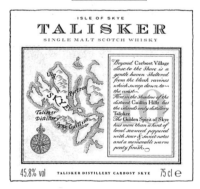

TALISKER 10-year-old, 45.8 vol

Colour Amber-red, bright.

Nose Pungent, smoke-accented, rounded.

Body Full, slightly syrupy.

Palate Smoky, malty-sweet, with sourness and a very big pepperiness developing.

Finish Very peppery, huge, long.

SCORE 90

TAMDHU

Distillery rating ☆☆☆ **Producer** Highland Distilleries
Region Highlands **District** Speyside

T HE PRINCIPAL SPEYSIDE PRODUCT among the bottled single malts in the Highlands Distilleries range. A mild, urbane, whisky, leaning toward malty sweetness.

The distillery is in the heart of Speyside, between Knockando and Cardhu. It was founded in 1896 and largely rebuilt in the 1970s. Water comes from the Tamdhu Burn, which flows through woodland into the Spey. Tamdhu has its own maltings, which are of the Saladin type. This was one of several malt distilleries that were served by a rural railway line up the Spey valley.

The whisky is becoming better known as a bottled single malt, and is a component of The Famous Grouse blend. At barrel proof, it has performed especially well in Scotch Malt Whisky Society bottlings.

TAMDHU Eight-year-old, 40 vol, Gordon and MacPhail

Colour Amber.

Nose Light, sweetish, malty. Some sherry character.

Body Light to medium.

Palate Sweetish, slightly toffeeish malt character, developing toward some peaty dryness.

Finish Smoky, then returning to malty sweetness.

SCORE 75

TAMDHU 10-year-old, 40 vol

Colour Pale amber.

Nose Perhaps a dash smokier.

Body Light to medium, rounded.

Palate Fragrant perfuminess. Toffeeish and malty, without being rich.

Finish Mellow, complete.

SCORE 75

TAMDHU 15-year-old, 43 vol

Colour Amber.

Nose Full, appetizing. Definite sherry character.

Body Light to medium, firm.

Palate Accent on malty sweetness, but with a nice balance of aromatic, cedary smokiness. Lots of character, but this becomes evident only after a period of acquaintance. This is a restrained, well balanced, malt.

Finish Beautifully rounded. A gentle after-dinner whisky.

SCORE 76

TAMNAVULIN

Distillery rating ☆☆☆   **Producer** Invergordon
Region Highland   **District** Speyside (Livet)

RIGHT ON THE LITTLE RIVER LIVET, on the steep side of the glen. Among the malts that are produced in the parish of Glenlivet, this is the lightest in body, though not in palate. In taste, it is a little more assertive than Tomintoul, with which it might be most closely compared.

The exact location of the distillery, the hamlet of Tomnavoulin, favours a different spelling from the distillery, but such discrepancies are hardly unusual in Scotland. The name means "mill on the hill", and part of the premises was formerly used for the carding of wool. The distillery, built in the 1960s, has a somewhat utilitarian look, but makes an elegant malt that is a delightful aperitif. Look out for occasional bottlings of especially good vintages under the rubric "Stillman's Dram".

TAMNAVULIN 10-year-old (no age statement), 43 vol

Colour Very pale, "white wine".
Nose Faint hint of peat. Oily, crushed barley perfume.
Body Light, smooth.
Palate Grassy, hint of lemon, perhaps also flowering currant.
Finish Aromatic.

SCORE 76

PRODUCT OF SCOTLAND
SINGLE MALT SCOTCH WHISKY
from
Tamnavulin-Glenlivet
Distillery
Proprietors:
Tamnavulin-Glenlivet Distillery Co. Ltd.

Bottled by Wm. Cadenhead,
75 cl   18 Golden Square, Aberdeen   46% vol
Scotland

TAMNAVULIN 20-year-old, 46 vol, Cadenhead (cask sample)

Colour Deep amber.

Nose Powerful sherry, with some dryness behind.

Body Light, to medium.

Palate Sherryish, gingery, lemony, sappy.

Finish Overwhelmingly sappy and oaky, even after considerable dilution.

SCORE 64

TEANINICH

Distillery rating ☆☆☆   **Producer** United Distillers
Region Highlands   **District** Northern Highlands

A WELL-MADE, ASSERTIVE malt in the earthy style of the Northern Highlands. The distillery, near Alness, north of the Cromarty Firth, was founded in 1817, grew very quickly, and was extended in 1899. In 1970, a new stillhouse was constructed. With its six stills visible from the road, it looks a very modern establishment. It closed in the mid 1980s but reopened in 1991, and there may be future official bottlings in the "flora and fauna" series.

TEANINICH 1975, 40 vol, Gordon and MacPhail (cask sample)

Colour Pale amber.

Nose Light, leafy, smokiness. Aromatic, appetizing.

Body Medium, soft, quite lush.

Palate Toffeeish, spicy.

Finish Dry, with a hint of leafy smokiness.

SCORE 72

TEANINICH 1982, 40 vol, Gordon and MacPhail (cask sample)

Colour Pale, "white wine".

Nose Malty, toffeeish, at first, then spicy and sharp.

Body Light to medium, but with some chewiness.

Palate Toffeeish start, becoming spicy, dry and sharp.

Finish Hint of leafy, smoky, dryness.

SCORE 70

TOBERMORY

Distillery rating ☆☆ **Producer** Tobermory Distillers
Region Highlands (Island) **District** Mull

THIS FAMOUS, VERY SMALL, old distillery, the only one on the island of Mull, reopened in 1990, after a decade's "silence".

It has continued to market two products: a malt and a blend. The former, identified as Tobermory The Malt Scotch Whisky, is presented in a bottle with an enamelled label. It is a vatted malt, containing some Tobermory whiskies of up to 20-years-old and proportions of newly-mature spirit from elsewhere. The latter has a conventional label, and is described as Tobermory blended Scotch Whisky. Single malts from this distillery have been bottled by the independents under the site's older name, Ledaig. These independent bottlings have much more island character.

Tobermory is the main village on Mull, and the home of the distillery. It is a dramatic location, at the foot of a steep hill, with the distillery signalling the beginning of the village, which spreads round a broad bay.

The distillery was founded in 1798 and the present buildings were erected during its first period of operation, which continued until 1826. The distillery was "silent" for long periods in the mid 1800s and mid 1900s, and was twice revived during the 1970s. Now it has been revived again.

With the growing interest in malts, the Tobermory distillery, on the coast of Mull, is becoming a tourist attraction.

TOBERMORY THE MALT, no age statement, 40 vol

Colour Full, gold.

Nose Peatiness – light, but definite. Also some sweetness.

Body Medium, soft.

Palate Dry, peaty, fruity, but not intense. The island character is there, but relatively restrained.

Finish Light, aromatic, becoming slightly sweeter.

SCORE 67

LEDAIG 18-year-old, 55.2 vol, James MacArthur (cask sample)

Colour Pale gold.

Nose Intense iodine, seaweed.

Body Medium, firm.

Palate Peppery, spicy, seaweedy, dry.

Finish Peppery.

SCORE 79

LEDAIG 1973, 40 vol, Gordon and MacPhail

Colour Amber-red.

Nose Intensely peaty.

Body Medium, firm.

Palate Peaty, phenolic, dry, intense. An excellent island malt.

Finish Powerful, peaty, peppery, warming, lingering.

SCORE 76

Other versions of Tobermory
The Scotch Malt Whisky Society found a "leathery" peatiness in a 10-year-old, at 60.2 vol, but this was much smoother and sweeter. SCORE 75.

TOMATIN

Distillery rating ☆☆☆   **Producer** Takara, Shuzo and Okura
Region Highlands   **District** Speyside (Findhorn)

THE FIRST SCOTTISH distillery to be wholly-owned by a Japanese company. A second Japanese company subsequently acquired Ben Nevis, and others have shareholdings in Scottish whisky companies.

Tomatin was established in 1897, but saw its great years of expansion between the 1950s and the 1970s. During this period, it became the biggest malt distillery in Scotland, and one of the largest in the world. It is just a little smaller than Suntory's Hakushu distillery.

As a very large distillery, Tomatin produced a broad-shouldered malt as a filler for countless blends during the boom years. It is neither the most complex nor the most assertive of malts, but it is far tastier than is widely realized. For the novice wishing to move from the lighter single malts to something a little more imposing, the climb to Tomatin is well worthwhile.

TOMATIN 10-year-old, 40 vol

Colour Full gold.

Nose Appetizingly fresh and clean, with a light, malty sweetness, and a hint of dry, perfumy smokiness.

Body Medium, soft, smooth.

Palate Sweet, but not overpoweringly so. Developing some gingery, perfumy, dryness.

Finish Slighty chewy.

SCORE 75

TOMATIN 13-year-old, 60.5 vol, Cadenhead

Colour Greeny gold.

Nose Fresh, slightly sharp.

Body Medium, soft.

Palate Sweet, toffeeish.

Finish Perfumy, dry.

SCORE 74

TOMATIN 1968, 40 vol, Gordon and MacPhail

Colour Full gold.

Nose Sweetish, malty, aromatic.

Body Medium, soft, lightly syrupy.

Palate Sweet, perfumy, fruity (orangey?).

Finish Rather quick.

SCORE 75

TOMATIN 1966, 46 vol, Signatory

Colour Bronze.

Nose Sweetish, malty, very aromatic.

Body Medium, soft, lightly syrupy.

Palate Sweetish, perfumy, toffeeish.

Finish Clinging toffee character.

SCORE 75

Other versions of Tomatin
A Gordon and MacPhail 1964 vintage (40 vol) is very dry – and
notably fruity, expecially in the nose. SCORE 74.

TOMINTOUL

Distillery rating ☆☆☆ **Producer** Whyte and Mackay
Region Highlands **District** Speyside (Livet)

TOMINTOUL (PRONOUNCED TOM-IN-T'OWL) is a village which is the base camp for climbers and walkers in the area around the rivers Avon and Livet. Nearby, Cromdale and the Ladder Hills foreshadow the Cairngorm Mountains. This is the high, remote Livet countryside that once abounded in illicit distilleries. Tomintoul itself had a good few.

It is a few miles from the village to the present distillery, which is on the edge of forest, close to the Avon but still within the parish of Glenlivet. The Tomintoul distillery was built in the 1960s, and is of a modern appearance.

Despite the wildness of the surroundings, the Livet malts are all characteristically elegant, and Tomintoul is very much in this style. In palate, Tomintoul is the lightest of the district's malts, though it has a little more body than its neighbours and contemporary, Tamnavulin.

TOMINTOUL 12-year-old, 43 vol
Colour Full gold.
Nose Delicate, slightly spirity, grassy, perfumy.
Body Light, soft smooth.
Palate Sweetish, notes of crushed barley, and maltiness.
Finish Lively and long-lasting.

SCORE 76

TORMORE

Distillery rating ☆☆☆ **Producer** Allied Distillers
Region Highlands **District** Speyside

ARCHITECTURALLY THE MOST elegant of all malt distilleries, and with a whisky of equal urbanity. As the hills around the Livet and Avon recede, after miles with barely a building, Tormore presents a sight that is hard to believe.

With its ornamental curling lake and fountains; its pristine, white buildings, decorative dormer windows, belfry and musical clock, the topiary, and the huge hill of dense firs forming a backdrop, Tormore might be a spa, offering a mountain water cure. Instead, it brings forth the water of life, *uisge beatha.* In its high, cold, location, shaded from the sun, it produces a beautifully clean malt.

Tormore was erected in 1958, during the boom years for the Scotch whisky industry. It was the first completely new malt distillery to be built in the Highlands in the 20th century, and was evidently intended as a showpiece. It was originally built by Long John Distillers, and designed by Sir Albert Richardson.

TORMORE Five-year-old, 43 vol

Colour Full gold.
Nose Clean, dry, faintly smoky. Toasted almonds?
Body Medium, firm.
Palate Appetizing. Teasing balance of clean, malty sweetness and faintly smoky dryness. Leans slightly toward sweetness.
Finish Smooth, very mellow for its youth.

SCORE 75

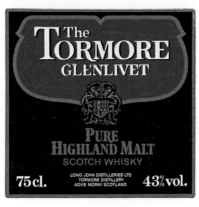

TORMORE 10-year-old, 43 vol

Colour Full gold.

Nose Slightly more almondy.

Body Medium, smooth – full texture.

Palate Soft, beautifully balanced.

Finish Soft, well rounded – and very long.

SCORE 76

TULLIBARDINE

Distillery rating ☆☆☆ **Producer** Invergordon
Region Highlands **District** Midlands

PRODUCT OF SCOTLAND

Tullibardine

SINGLE HIGHLAND MALT
SCOTCH WHISKY

*A Single Malt Scotch Whisky of quality
and distinction distilled and bottled by*
TULLIBARDINE DISTILLERY LIMITED
BLACKFORD   PERTHSHIRE   SCOTLAND

40%vol   70cl

SOUTH OF PERTH, and half way to Stirling, this is a southerly distillery, but still north of the Highland line. The location, Blackford, is noted for its well-water, and once produced famous ales. It was on the site of a former brewery that the Tullibardine distillery opened in 1949. In the 1970s, it was taken over by Invergordon and largely rebuilt. Tullibardine is available as a bottled single malt with the distillery label. The principal bottling is a 10-year-old, though other ages can sometimes be found.

Tullibardine is not an especially well-known malt, but in its own mild-mannered way it makes a pleasant, tasty, pre-dinner companion.

TULLIBARDINE 10-year-old, 40 vol

Colour Gold.

Nose Soft, malty, sweetish.

Body Medium, firm, smooth.

Palate Full, with clean, grassy-malty sweetness. Only medium-sweet. Develops to a fruity, almost Chardonnay-like wineyness.

Finish Sweetish, fragrant, appetizing, big.

SCORE 76

SINGLE GRAIN WHISKIES

A review of malts cannot include single grain whiskies, which are another species, but they merit an appendix. These two types of whisky do, after all, live together in a married state in every bottle of blended Scotch. While the malts provide the fullness of character in the blend, there is usually more grain whisky in the bottle.

Because it is made in a continuous process, in a column-shaped still, grain whisky can be produced more quickly and cheaply. It has less character, but it still takes some flavour from its principal raw material, whether unmalted barley, wheat or corn (maize). It is a whisky, not a neutral spirit, and it is aged for at least three years. There are eight grain distilleries operating in Scotland, and one or two more that are silent.

For decades, United Distillers and its predecessor D.C.L. have bottled as a single grain the product of its Cameronbridge Distillery, in Fife. This is made available – almost as a curiosity – but not actively marketed, as Cameron Brig, with no age statement, over the Haig name. It has an amber colour and hints of sherry and caramel to round out the grainy palate.

In more recent years, a single grain from Invergordon distillery, in the Northern Highlands, has been actively marketed, at 10 years old, by the company of the same name. The design of the label, and the advertising, suggests that this is aimed at fashion-conscious young drinkers, perhaps in the worthy hope of weaning them off vodka.

There have been several independent bottlings of much older single grains, some from now-defunct distilleries. Signatory has a perfumy, woody, quite full, single grain from Dumbarton and a sweeter one from North British. James MacArthur has a woody, sherryish, Carsebridge, and softer, rounder, examples from Ben Nevis and Lochside.

These are bottlings for the lover of esoteric drinks.

The Invergordon Single Grain has a golden colour and a soft, clean, sweetish palate.

VATTED MALTS

Why produce a whisky that is neither a single malt nor altogether a blend? It is argued that, while a single may vary according to vintage or season, a vatted malt can be more consistent. Are lovers of malts afflicted by an obsession with consistency? Perhaps the idea is attractive to importers, distributors or retailers who want their own malt label. At one point the vatted product was perhaps also seen as an introductory step into the world of malts. Today, with the growing popularity of the singles, less is heard of vatted malts.

The best-known is probably *Strathconon* 12-year-old, produced under the Buchanan label by United Distillers. This is described as being vatted from four malts, chosen "one for bouquet, another for flavour, a third for body, the last for its ability to blend all four into a balanced, mellow, flavour." It has a bright, full gold colour; an appetizing, clean, malty-fruity nose; a soft, medium body; a dry, malty palate; and a dry finish. A very pleasant malt.

Another example from United Distillers, this time under the Haig label, is *Glenleven.* This is identified as a Highland malt, and said to be vatted from six singles. It has a fuller, bronze colour; a hint of peat in its spicy nose; a light to medium, slightly oily body; a malty-smoky palate, and a big, warming, long, dry finish. Quite a characterful whisky.

Where a distillery has ceased to operate, it may keep its label alive by producing a vatted malt. This is true of Glen Flager. This was a Lowland single malt produced at Moffat, near Airdrie, in the mid 1960s and 1970s. In the mid 1980s the distillery was dismantled, but the label has been continued on a vatted malt. For the moment a proportion of the light-bodied Glen Flagler single malt is being used in the fuller-tasting vatted product. The vatted product, *Glen Flagler Pure Malt Special Reserve,* has a gold colour; both dryness and sweetness in the nose; a soft, sticky body; a sweetish palate; and a slightly resiny finish.

The best use of the vatted malt is that devised by Gordon and MacPhail. Among an interesting range of its own vattings, this company has a series, principally at 12 years old, devoted to some of the classic regions and districts, see opposite.

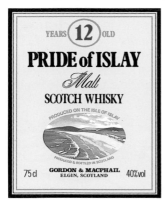

PRIDE OF THE LOWLANDS
This has an amber colour; a lightly smoky nose (a dash of Glenkinchie?); a light, soft, smooth body; a sweetish, aromatic (a hint of grassiness, or linseed?), palate; and some sherry in the finish. Almost too characterful for today's Lowland selection.

PRIDE OF STRATHSPEY
This standard 12-year-old has an amber colour; a hint of flowering currant in the nose; a medium to full body; a sweet, sherryish, palate; and a smooth, malty finish. A 25-year-old *Pride of Strathspey* has a slightly fuller colour; a firmer body; a drier nose, with a hint of smokiness; more smokiness in the palate; and a dry, smoky finish.

PRIDE OF ISLAY
A product that has a fairly full amber colour; light to medium peatiness in the nose; a medium to full body; some iodine and sappiness in the palate; and a long, peaty, dry sherryish finish. Very dry and assertive.

PRIDE OF ORKNEY
This has an amber-red colour; a heather-honey nose; a medium-to-full, smooth body; a complex, heathery, peaty palate; and a long, warming, dryish finish.

OTHER SINGLE MALTS

These are single malts, but not single-malt *Scotches,* made in Ireland and Japan. They are well-made products produced in a similar style to those from Scotland. No single malts are produced anywhere else in the world, though some malts are bottled in other countries.

IRELAND

Bushmills Malt, at 10-years-old, from County Antrim, Ireland, has a full gold colour; a warm, sweet nose, with some linseed; a very soft body; a sweetish, oily, malty palate; and a soft, smooth, dryish finish. Surprisingly, it has less of an obvious sherry character than its de luxe blend partner, *Black Bush.* These whiskeys, and the regular *Old Bushmills,* are triple distilled. The Bushmills distillery, in the little town of the same name, was licensed by King James I in 1608. It is the world's oldest licensed malt distillery, though its single was launched only in the mid 1980s.

Home of the only single malt Irish Whiskey, Bushmills Distillery, with its pagodas reflected in its dam, is a distinctive landmark.

JAPAN

It was also during the 1980s that the Japanese malt distilleries began to bottle single malts.

The best-known example is produced at Suntory's oldest distillery, founded in 1923, amid the red and black pines, bamboo groves, and three rivers of the Yamazaki Valley, between Osaka and Kyoto. *Yamazaki Pure Malt Whisky* has a pale colour; a fresh, clean, malty nose; a light to medium body; a crisp, dry, malty palate; and a long, soft, malty, warming finish.

A second Japanese single malt is made by the smaller company Sanraku Ocean, at a tiny, pretty, overgrown, distillery founded in the 1930s in the mountain resort of Karuizawa, after which it takes its name. *Karuizawa Fine Aged Straight Malt Whisky* has a pale colour; a sherryish nose; a light, slightly oily body; a clean, malty, sweet palate; and a crisp finish.

The newest entrant from Japan, *Nikka "Hokkaido" Single Malt,* has an amber-red colour; a dry nose; a medium to full body; a dry, malty, sherryish palate, with some chewiness; and a very smooth, mild, sweetish finish. This distinctive malt is produced at Nikka's oldest distillery, on the island of Hokkaido. The founder of Nikka studied on Speyside from 1918, and the small distillery, in the seaside town of Yoichi, is a handsome tribute to its inspirations.

The distinctive rooftops and stone buildings of the Nikka distillery.

Hakushu is the largest malt distillery in the world.

STORING AND SERVING SINGLE MALTS

Malt whisky is a drink to contemplate, and certainly not one to rush. As with fine wine, the way a malt is served can add to or detract from the enjoyment of drinking it. To make sure malts are enjoyed to the full, therefore, it is worth bearing mind a few points, which I have outlined below.

Temperature
A malt in its natural state will throw an unattractive haze if it is refrigerated. That is why the commercial versions are filtered at cold temperatures. This chill-filtration removes solids that might otherwise precipitate – but also strips out some texture and tase. There is no reason to store malts at low temperatures, and every reason to avoid chilling them or adding ice. Cold numbs the tongue, and ice brings about changes in the malt. Whisky most fully expresses itself if it is stored and served at room temperature. A single malt is not meant to be a cold, thirst-quenching, drink.

Glassware
With its no-nonsense shape, and refraction of the light through the colours of the drink, the traditional cut-glass tumbler is aesthetically pleasing. Where it fails is in presenting the colour naturally, and – more important – in retaining the aroma. These two requirements favour the use of a brandy-type "snifter glass" for single malts, and this is becoming more popular. Whisky blenders do their tasting in a similar glass designed for their purpose. It is in the style of a tall, narrow, snifter or an elongated sherry copita.

Dilution
The texture – but not necessarily the aroma and palate – of the fuller-bodied style of malt is best appreciated if it is sampled undiluted. A good compromise is to add just the odd drop of water, "like the dew on a rose", in the words of whisky merchant and writer Wallace Milroy. A small amount of water will help awaken the bouquet of a malt, and bring out aromatics in the palate. Some professional blenders work only with their nose, not finding it necessary to let the whisky pass their lips. Others like to sample the whisky undiluted, though this can soon anaesthetize the palate. Some blenders like to dilute 50-50, using distilled, or very pure, water.

INDEPENDENT BOTTLINGS

Despite the increase in the number of malts being released as singles by distilleries, independent bottlings are also becoming more widely available. While official bottlings are normally reduced from a cask strength of 60-plus to around 40 vol, with varying degrees of filtration at cold temperatures to ensure brightness, some independents avoid these steps, believing that they remove flavour. *The Scotch Malt Whisky Society* (The Vaults, Leith, Edinburgh, tel: 031-554 3452) is dedicated to this view.

Old established independents *Gordon and MacPhail* still operates the small-town grocery and whisky shop with which its business began (at 58-60 South Street, Elgin, tel: 0343 545111), but is far better known as a wholesaler. Its high stock levels ensure some continuity of availability of particular malts, with some consistency of style. *Cadenhead* retails through a whisky shop at 172 Canongate, on the Royal Mile, Edinburgh (tel: 031-556 5864), but wholesales from Springbank (tel: 0586 52085). Cadenhead does mainly single-cask bottlings, so vintages may differ substantially. These are not chill-filtered.

New companies *James MacArthur* (with a phone number in High Wycombe, England: 04945-30740), and Edinburgh-based *Signatory* (tel: 031-657 4173) both bottle without chill-filtration. Alcohol content of these bottlings vary, but they are usually at cask strength.

American market *Prime Malt* is a series name for a range of usually-sherryish malts from Carlton Importers, of Baltimore, Maryland. *Michel Couvreur,* of Meldrum House, Aberdeenshire, offers in the U.S. a range of single-cask malts of varying character.

"Branded" malts Some single malts bear names that sound like distilleries but, in fact, are not. These are brand-names created by importers or retailers, who may at any time change their source of supply according to availability or price. For that reason, they are not included in this book.

VISITING THE DISTILLERIES

There was a time when many malt distilleries did not even have a bottle of their product on the premises, or a licence to offer a glass to visitors. However, as interest in single malts has grown, so has the number of distilleries that are formally organised to welcome visitors. Many now have what they call "visitor reception centres", sometimes showing a video on the production process, almost always offering a guided tour, usually with a tasting at the end, perhaps with a gift-shop, sometimes a bar or restaurant. Even distilleries that do not formally offer tours will often welcome visitors.

A number of well-known Highland distilleries with reception centres have organised themselves into a Malt Whisky Trail for the benefit of visitors. A booklet and map can be obtained from the Scottish Tourist Board, at Ravelstone Crescent, Edinburgh (Tel: 031-332 2433) and some other Scottish tourist offices.

Visitors to Edinburgh can view the history of the industry from the comfort of a motorised cask at The Scotch Whisky Heritage Centre, at 358 Castlehill, on the Royal Mile, Edinburgh. The Cairngorm Whisky Centre and Museum (Tel: 0479 810574) is in Aviemore, Scotland's main skiing centre. Visitors who would like to wander freely in a perfectly preserved, unmodernised, distillery should see Dallas Dhu, near Forres (Information: Historic Scotland, 20 Brandon Street, Edinburgh. Tel: 031-244 3101).

The following distilleries are willing to show visitors around. Some of them have reception centres and shops, but many are ordinary working distilleries and a telephone call in advance is advisable. The usual opening hours are 9.30 am to 4 pm Monday-Friday. Some distilleries are open all year round; others only open in the summer months.

ABERFELDY
Aberfeldy, Perthshire
0887 20330
(Visitors' centre)

ABERLOUR
Aberlour, Banffshire
0340 871204
(Visitors' centre)

AUCHROISK
Mulben, Banffshire
05426 333

AULTMORE
Keith, Banffshire
05422 2762

BALBLAIR
Edderton, Tain
08628 2273

BALMENACH
Cromdale, Grantown-on-Spey,
Morayshire
0479 2569

BEN NEVIS
Fort William, Inverness-shire,
0397 70 2476
(Visitors' centre)

BENRIACH
Longmorn, Elgin, Morayshire
05422 7471

BENRINNES
Aberlour, Banffshire
03405 215

BLADNOCH
Bladnoch, Wigtownshire
09884 2235
(Visitors' centre)

BLAIR ATHOL
Pitlochry, Perthshire
0796 2234
(Visitors' centre)

BOWMORE
Bowmore, Islay, Argyll
04968 1441
(Visitors' centre)

BRUICHLADDICH
Bruichladdich, Islay, Argyll
04968 5221
(Visitors' centre)

BUNNAHABHAIN
Port Askaig, Islay, Argyll
04968 4646

CAOL ILA
Port Askaig, Islay, Argyll
04968 4207
(Visitors' centre)

CARDHU
Cardhu, Morayshire
03406 204
(Visitors' centre)

CLYNELISH
Brora, Sutherland
40482 1444
(Visitors' centre)

CRAGGANMORE
Ballindalloch, Banffshire
08072 202

CRAIGELLACHIE
Craigellachie, Banffshire
03404 212/228

DAILUAINE
Carron, Aberlour, Banffshire
03406 361/362

DALLAS DHU (not in production)
Forres, Morayshire
031 244 3101
(Visitors' centre)

DALMORE
Alness, Rothshire
0349 882 362

DALWHINNIE
Dalwhinnie, Inverness-shire
05282 264

DUFFTOWN
Dufftown, Keith, Banffshire
0340 20224/20773

EDRADOUR
Pitlochry, Perthshire
07962 095
(Visitors' centre)

FETTERCAIRN
Fettercairn, Kincardineshire
05614 244
(Visitors' centre)

GLENALLACHIE
Abelour, Banffshire
0340 871 315

GLENBURGIE
Forres, Morayshire
03438 5258

GLENCADAM
Brechin, Angus
03562 2217

GLENDRONACH
Forgue, By Huntly,
Aberdeenshire
0406 682 202
(Visitors' centre)

GLENDULLAN
Dufftown, Banffshire
0340 20 250

GLEN ELGIN
Longmorn, Morayshire
03438 6212
(Visitors' centre)

GLENFARCLAS
Marypark, Ballindalloch,
Banffshire
08072 257
(Visitors' centre)

GLENFIDDICH
Dufftown, Banffshire
03402 0373
(Visitors' centre)

GLENGOYNE
Dumgoyne, Stirlingshire
041 332 6361
(Visitors' centre)

GLEN GRANT
Rothes, Morayshire
05422 7471
(Visitors' centre)

GLENKINCHIE
Pencaitland, Tranent,
East Lothian
0875 340333
(Visitors' centre)

THE GLENLIVET
Minmore, Banffshire
05422 7471
(Visitors' centre)

GLENLOSSIE
By Elgin, Morayshire
03438 6331

GLENMORANGIE
Tain, Ross-shire
0862 892043

GLEN MORAY
Elgin, Morayshire
0343 542577

GLEN ORD
Muir of Ord, Ross-shire
0463 870421
(Visitors' centre)

GLEN SCOTIA
Campbeltown, Argyll
0586 52288

GLEN SPEY
Rothes, Morayshire
05426 333

GLENTURRET
Crieff, Perthshire
0764 2424,
(Visitors' centre)

HIGHLAND PARK
Kirkwall, Orkney
0856 3107
(Visitors' centre)

INCHGOWER
Buckie, Banffshire
0542 31161

INVERLEVEN
Dumbarton, Dumbarton-shire
038965 111

ISLE OF JURA
Craighouse, Jura, Argyll
04968 2240

KNOCKANDO
Knockando, Morayshire
05426 333

KNOCKDHU
Knock, Banffshire
046686 223

LAGAVULIN
Port Ellen, Islay, Argyll
0496 2250/2400
(Visitors' centre)

LAPHROAIG
Port Ellen, Islay, Argyll
0496 2418
(Visitors' centre)

LINKWOOD
Elgin, Morayshire
0343 547004

LOCHSIDE
Montrose, Tayside
0674 72 737

THE MACALLAN
Craigellachie, Banffshire
03408 71471

MILTONDUFF
Elgin, Morayshire
0343 547433

MORTLACH
Dufftown, Keith, Banffshire
0340 20318

OBAN
Stafford Street, Oban, Argyll
0631 62110
(Visitors' centre)

ORD
See Glen Ord

PITTYVAICH
Dufftown, Keith, Banffshire
0340 20561

PULTENEY
Wick, Caithness
09552 371

ROSEBANK
Falkirk, Stirlingshire
0324 23325

ROYAL LOCHNAGAR
Crathie, Ballater, Aberdeenshire
03397 42273
(Visitors' centre)

SCAPA
Kirkwall, Orkney
0856 2071

SINGLETON OF AUCHROISK
See under Auchroisk

SPEYBURN
Rothes, Morayshire
03403 213

STRATHISLA
Keith, Banffshire
05422 7471
(Visitors' centre)

TALISKER
Carbost, Isle of Skye
047842 203

TAMDHU
Knockando, Morayshire
03406 221
(Visitors' centre)

TAMNAVULIN
Ballindalloch, Dumbartonshire
08073 442
(Visitors' centre)

TOMATIN
Tomatin, Inverness-shire
08082 234
(Visitors' centre)

TORMORE
Grantown-on-Spey, Morayshire
08075 244

INDEX

FURTHER READING

The World Guide to Whisky
by Michael Jackson (1987)

The Schweppes Guide to
Scotch *by Philip Morrice* (1983)

The Making of Scotch Whisky
*by Michael Moss and
John Hume* (1981).

The Century Companion to
Whiskies *by Derek Cooper*
(1978/83)

And some earlier classics:

The Whiskies of Scotland
by R. J. S. McDowall

Scotch Whisky
by David Daiches

Scotch
by Sir Robert Bruce Lockhart

The Whisky Distilleries of
the United Kingdom
by Alfred Barnard

ACKNOWLEDGMENTS

My thanks once again to all the people whose assistance was acknowledged in the first edition of this book, and to the following:

For their help in tracking down some of the most offbeat products mentioned in this book, I would like to thank The Bloomsbury Wine and Spirit Company, London (John Anderson and Brian Iles), and The Whisky Shop, in Glasgow and various other cities (Mike Batchelor). The bar at the Athenaeum Hotel, Piccadilly, London, has also helped keep my taste-buds exercised between bouts of research. In New York, I have often tasted unusual vintages at The North Star Pub, South Street, Seaport (my thanks to Deven Black) and Keen's Chophouse (Rick Brook – and his predecessor Dan Beck).

Gordon and MacPhail have helped me track down malts far beyond their own bottlings, and I especially thank Ian and David Urquhart for assistance. My thanks, also to Gordon Wright and colleagues at Cadenhead's; Arthur Winning at James MacArthur; and Brian Symington at Signatory. Not for the first time, I owe thanks to Yvonne Scott, at the Scotch Malt Whisky Association; Russell Sharp and colleagues at the Scotch Malt Whisky Society; Penny Clifton, at Phipps Public Relations; and Hilary Laidlaw Thomson, of Media Relations – MJ

Dorling Kindersley would like to thank the following for their help in preparing the first edition of this book: Toni Rann, Candida Ross-MacDonald, James Allen and Simonne Waud. Second edition prepared by: Victoria Sorzano (editor), Philip Lord (designer), Helen Creeke (production), Steve Gorton (extra label photography).

Photography All photography by Ian Howes except: title page, Stephen Oliver; p.10 bottom left, Glenmorangie Distillery Ltd.; p.78 Campbell Distillers Ltd.; and p. 229 Tetsuya Fukui.

Maps produced by Lovell Johns Limited, Oxford.
Typeset in ITC Garamond by Dataserve Associates, Milton Keynes.
Reproduction by Columbia Offset (UK) Limited.